How To Fail Everything

A comprehensive guide.

While every precaution has been taken in the preparation of this book, the publisher assumes no responsibility for errors or omissions, or for damages resulting from the use of the information contained herein.

HOW TO FAIL AT PRACTICALLY EVERYTHING: A COMPREHENSIVE GUIDE

First edition. November 8, 2023.

Copyright © 2023 Jesse Lucas.

ISBN: 979-8223824091

Written by Jesse Lucas.

Table of Contents

How To Fail At Practically Everything: A Comprehensive Guide 1
Introduction 2
Chapter 1 7
Chapter 2 16
Chapter 3 26
Chapter 4 37
Chapter 5 47
Chapter 6 56
Chapter 7 67
Chapter 8 78
Chapter 9 87

Jesse Lucas

Introduction

J.K. Rowling, Michael Jordan, Albert Einstein, Abraham Lincoln, George Lucas, Walt Disney, The Beatles, Thomas Edison, Winston Churchill, Jesse Lucas. At first glance of this list of names most people would probably see a connection with all of them. Except for the last name, my name. And that would be for good reason too. Every single individual on this list has achieved great accomplishments whether it is for entertainment, physical accolades, or political success. Except for me.

So you may be asking yourself "why did he include himself on this list"? I'm not a successful author, business man, entertainer, musician, and despite my love of sports, I am about the furthest thing from being an athlete. So why the inclusion? Despite the apparent distance in stature between myself and the other individuals on this list, I believe the list is whole and completely intact as is. This is a list of individuals who have failed. And failed. And failed again. And when they thought they finally got it right they failed again.

"Success is not final, failure is not fatal: It is the courage to continue that counts." Winston Churchill is probably one of my favorite historical figures. He rose up at a time when no one else would. Looked evil directly in the eyes when no one else did. And told Hitler he could shove "Mein Kampf" promptly up "Sienen Hintern". Go ahead, Google the German. Ok, now that you are back and probably at least slightly smirked or chuckled, let's continue. So he may not have said those words exactly. But he was really one of the only major leaders that stood up to the overwhelming power of Nazi Germany. He also had many (let me channel my inner brit) bloody brilliant one liners that I can only aspire to match in my life. Lady Astor once told him that "If I was your wife I would put poison in your coffee". To which Churchill replied "If I were married to you, I would drink it". Although I greatly aspire to Churchill's wit, I greatly admire his stubbornness to quit. In 1915 Britain set out on the Gallipoli Campaign during WWI. It was a disaster. Churchill backed this plan from the very beginning. The final results were a total of more than 250,000 casualties including about 46,000 dead. By comparison there were an estimated 10,000 allied troops killed for day one of the invasion of D-day. But Churchill didn't stay down. He came back and I believe saved the world. I don't think many other people would have had the sheer gall to stand up in the face of such powerful evil, and hold out for the end. No matter what the end looked like for him.

"Success is failure in progress." The word Einstein is synonymous with intelligence. I believe it even contributed to Kevin, Meredith, Kelly, and Erin winning the trivia contest (I have to throw in "The Office" references whenever possible). But the man that most people regard as one of the most intelligent to ever live could not speak fluently until he was 9 years old. He ended up getting expelled from school and was refused admittance to the Zurich Polytechnic School. Einstein went on to win the Nobel Prize in Physics in 1921 and his research has influenced nearly every part of our lives today.

"I've missed more than 9,000 shots in my career. I've lost almost 300 games. 26 times, I've been trusted to take the game winning shot and missed. I've failed over and over and over again in my life. And that is why I succeed." A lot of people know the famous story of Michael Jordan. While still in high school he was cut from the basketball team. The story goes that he went home, locked himself in his room, and cried. Michael Jordan ended up going to college at North Carolina. There he led the Tar Heels to a National Championship. He was then drafted in 1984 by the Chicago Bulls. Jordan's individual accolades include 6 NBA Finals MVP awards, 10 scoring titles, 5 MVP awards, 10 All-NBA First Team designations, 9 All-Defensive First Team honors, 14 NBA All-Star selections, 3 All-Star Game MVP awards, 3 Steals titles, and the 1988 NBA Defensive Player of the Year award. He holds the title for highest career regular season scoring average, and highest career playoff scoring average. In 1999 he was named the greatest North American athlete of the 20th century by ESPN and was second to Babe Ruth on the Associated Press' list of athletes of the century. Not to mention being an integral part in helping Bugs Bunny defeat the Monstars and save the planet (I was a young Bulls fan so this was awesome to me at the time).

"We don't look backwards for very long. We keep moving forward, opening up new doors, and doing new things because we're curious... and curiosity keeps leading us down new paths." Walt Disney's success is one we probably experience the most in our culture. Disney is literally everywhere and owns companies and names like ESPN, Lucasfilm, Marvel, ABC, Pixar, Hollywood Records, and Touchstone Pictures. But it all started quite differently for Walt

Disney. He Dropped out of school on a failed attempt at joining the army. Helped start a company (Laugh-o-Gram Studios) that went bankrupt due to his lack of ability to run a successful business. Then he was fired from a newspaper in Missouri because he "lacked imagination, and had no original ideas." Yet today one of the most iconic Characters in history is none other than Mickey Mouse. And the company that shares his name is responsible for some of the most memorable childhood classics we all knew and loved growing up.

Another aspect I want to examine as we work through this book is biblical examples. I believe firmly that the Bible is just as much for us today as it has ever been for anyone in history. That being said, many of the lessons I have learned through the various experiences I will outline going forward have deep roots in biblical values. From David, Solomon, Samson, Saul, and many more. From Genesis to Revelation. I think there are very strong, tried and true principles in the pages of that book that can and will change your life if you give it the opportunity to.

Now, I am not going to get into a theological debate with anyone (although I really do love a good theological debate). No matter what your beliefs on The Bible are, it is a historical document and most scholars would agree that it is a correct historical document. Its stories can be backed up with other sources of history. But beyond all of that, the principles taught in it are just good principles. Be wise with your money, if you want to make friends then be friendly. Really solid and sometimes simple lessons and ideas that we have really gotten away from in our society. I strongly believe that no matter what your opinion of The Bible is, there are lessons that can be learned from it that will change your life.

So as I go through each of these biblical stories I will give an overview of the specific details of the story that pertain to the topic at hand. But I will also cite chapter and verse where the story can be found in The Bible. I would like to encourage anyone who has not read these stories in The Bible to please do so outside of just what is listed in this book.

Some of what I am bringing up in this book may not be what some would consider a failure, Some may just be a difficult situation that I was able to learn from. But, I believe there is a lesson that can be learned in all the situations I am going to bring up. Now let's get back to the list I brought up originally. I am not saying that I'm about to make it big, or that I will one day achieve the level of success that any of these individuals have had. But I can relate with their struggles. I can relate with repeated failure. Trying over and over and over again. Thinking I finally got it figured out only to fail again. I feel I have learned a lot through these experiences and from being around people who hold the same view. People who are not afraid of failure. I actually switched to a new job while in the process of writing this book and I loved seeing the thoughts of one of the new managers I have. She will very boldly and honestly say fail simply means First Attempt In Learning. Now I know she did not coin this phrase, but she really has taken it to heart and I believe it has served her and the company I now work for well.

In this book I want to take you on a journey. I want to look at experiences from my own life, and pull what I've learned from each of those. But I also want to look at stories of people who are not currently where I am. People who have made it to the other side. People who have reached such extreme levels of success that they (in some cases) have changed the world. I want to help people discover something that I myself am still discovering. I want to help people learn how to fail. Not give up. Not quit. Not Stop trying. But fail, learn, repeat. Until you reach success.

I feel this may be of common practice going forward in this book, but I want to address something before continuing. I am going to be bringing up several famous or influential people in this book. I will be examining their lives, looking at how they turned a failure (or perceived failure) into success. However this does not mean that I agree with every aspect of their lives or every decision they make. This is something we need to really get a hold of in this generation. People are flawed, all people, for all of time. That means that when someone does something great, that person is a flawed person.

Martin Luther King Jr. did a lot of great things for America and the world. He helped us get past a lot (not all) of the racial injustice going on in our country. But there is also a good bit of evidence that MLK was a pretty big sexist. Even standing by while a friend of his sexually assaulted a woman. (Bostock, 2019)

Oh and that path that MLK took us down, that path was started by Thomas Jefferson. Thomas Jefferson who was a slave owner. Thomas Jefferson who was originally going to outlaw slavery in the constitution, but didn't because he knew the southern states at the time would not sign on. And if we were going to gain independence we needed to work together. So instead he phrased it so that eventually there would be no alternative except for our country to finally confront the atrocity that is slavery. The simple phrase "We hold these truths to be self-evident, that ALL men are created equal" Not all white men. Most people do not know that Thomas Jefferson was publicly opposed to the international slave trade. He privately pushed for gradual emancipation and colonization of all slaves in the United States. And in 1807, as president, Thomas Jefferson signed a law prohibiting the importation of slaves into any port or place within the jurisdiction of the United States. Lin-Manuel Miranda must have forgotten that while portraying him as an avid slavery loving racist on broadway. My family and I actually really enjoy this musical. It is very entertaining, just not very historically factual.

So we can agree with something a person does or thinks without signing off on their entire life. That needs to be understood going forward. Not only in this book, but in our lives. I think this is one step we can all take that would make the world a much better place.

Chapter 1

<u>Tune Out Everyone, Except the Ones You Can't.</u>

I have always had this fascination with back stories. In pretty much everything I like; I want to know more. More about the person I am seeing and the why behind the what that I'm being exposed to. I have also always been drawn to music. I can play several instruments, I can sing, and I've even recorded some songs of my own. If I love a song I'll sit (sometimes go for hours, days, or even weeks) just trying to piece together what exactly the song is about. I will flip flop back and forth in my head sometimes arguing with myself over the deep unknown meaning behind the curtain of words or lyrics. I may see if I could find the artist talking about the inspiration of the song, or for that matter giving any kind of back story at all. So I decided that the best place to start this journey was with the music industry.

It really does not matter that Dick Rowe ended up being the guy who signed the Rolling Stones. He will probably forever be known as "the guy who passed on the Beatles". That's right, **THOSE** Beatles. John, Paul, George, and Pete (it was prior to Ringo) were turned down by the Decca recording company who said "We don't like their sound, and Guitar music is on its way out". Now some of the details of the story differ depending on who is telling it, but the main point remains the same. Before they made it famous, they were rejected. And rejected in a pretty big way.

On January 1st, 1962 the Beatles were auditioning for Decca. They had played a show several nights before and had not played well enough to land the deal. They had, however, played well enough to land a second chance. The New Year's day audition in London. They were told they needed to use Decca's amplifiers because their personal equipment was substandard. They took a little over an hour and recorded 15 songs in total.

Now Dick Rowe later recalled that he had instructed another individual to choose between the Beatles and a group called Brian Poole and the Tremeloes. They both sounded good. But one was a local group. The other was from Liverpool. So they decided to go with the local group, since it would be easier to work with them on a regular basis.

But all was not lost. After the audition the Beatles had some good recordings that made it easier to pitch the band to other labels. The Beatles did end up signing with a subsidiary of EMI via George Martin. Martin is also the one who brought up concerns about Pete's drumming which eventually led to Ringo Star joining the group in place of Pete Best. So you could make the argument that if not for the rejection, the world would have never known the Beatles. Or at least would have never known the Beatles as we remember them today. Regardless of if you like their music or not, you really can't argue against the impact they ended up having on culture and the music industry as a whole.

One thing that really stands out to me with this story is that they didn't really even seem fazed by the rejection. As a musician myself, I can say it is one of the most vulnerable things you can do to have someone judge your original work. Taking something that you have created. Something you are passionate about. Something you Love. And allowing someone else to judge that. I have felt that rejection and it is not nice. It down right sucks! Now I am sure the Beatles felt some of that as well. But seeing that they stuck with it, and ended up making a change for the positive of the band and landed a record deal. I think it's a good example of why you shouldn't let others' opinions of you affect your perception of yourself.

I believe there is someone in a biblical story that parallels this really well. He is one that many people are familiar with, maybe by name recognition only, even if they are not familiar at all with The Bible. The person I am speaking of is King David. But in order to tell the story we are going to start off before he was King.

I do want to make something clear with the biblical stories that I will be sharing. I may use some direct quotes where I feel it's needed to really emphasize a point, or get the meaning across. But for most of them I will be summarizing or paraphrasing. That being said, it bears repeating that I will reference where in The Bible each of these stories take place and I would encourage you to go read them in their entirety from the original source. I can honestly say your life could be changed forever by really digging into these stories and seeing the truth that lies in them.

So the first King of Israel was named Saul. After being God's choice Saul started doing things wrong. Specifically not being obedient to different orders God had given. Because of this God decided he is going to move on from Saul as King. So God speaks to Samuel, who was a prophet, and tells Samuel to go to the house of Jesse (Great name) and there he will find who to anoint to become the next King.

This story picks up in 1 Samuel 16:6. So Jesse is bringing his sons out in front of Samuel and Samuel is trying to decide which one will be the next King of Israel. He sees the first son (Eliab) and instantly thinks this must be the guy! I mean he does look so incredibly kingly already. Tall and Handsome (These are also things that people thought about Saul). But God told Samuel "Do not look at his appearance or at the height of his stature, because I have rejected him; for God sees not as man sees, for man looks at the outward appearance, but the Lord looks at the heart". Then Jesse calls his son Abinadab, but The Lord had not chosen him either. Then Jesse called Shammah, but The Lord had not called him either. This would continue until 7 sons had been brought before Samuel and none were chosen by God.

So Samuel asks Jesse "Are these all your sons". I love the reply here by Jesse. He answers "There remains yet the youngest, and behold, he is tending the sheep." Then Samuel tells Jesse to go send for his youngest son.

Now the story goes on to tell how when David did finally arrive God told Samuel that David was in fact the next King of Israel. Samuel anoints David and that starts him on the path towards becoming the greatest earthly King Israel would ever know. But this is an excellent example of rejection. I mean, David was completely overlooked by someone very close to him. His father knew he could handle their flock's out in the field (which we know involves killing bears and lions) but David was an afterthought when considering his sons for the role of king. Now to Jesse's credit, I think everyone would have probably made the same decisions. When talking about the next king, most people would have the same or similar criteria. The real focus here should be that God does not judge the same way that we do. God does not look for the same qualifications that we do. On the contrary. A common theme throughout the Bible is God choosing people who do not measure up in our eyes and by our standards. That way we can know, beyond all doubt, that it was God who did it.

Looking at David's life in more detail shows us that it wasn't all success. There are the peaks that most people are familiar with, but there were also many deep valleys in between. He has gone through a whole ordeal with Saul to finally become king of Israel. He has had some major successes along the way as well. But he has just recently had a major misstep. But first I would like to point out that one of my favorite things about the bible is that it is honest. Completely honest. Even with the heroes. We know they are human, they make mistakes, and because of that I believe we can know that they are real, and we should not disqualify ourselves from God's service simply because we messed up.

During a time where David was supposed to be out in the field with his soldiers he is staying behind in the city. While here he notices a woman named Bathsheba who is bathing on her roof. He's completely mesmerized by her, ends up having her brought to him and gets her pregnant. Now Bathsheba is actually married to a man named Uriah and Uriah is a soldier.

So once Bathsheba tells David she is pregnant he starts trying to cover it up. First he calls for Uriah to be brought before him. Once there he asks how the troops are, the state of the war, and things like that, then sends Uriah to go home to his wife. David assumes that Uriah's return from the battlefield would result in him and his wife being intimate, in which case Uriah would unknowingly claim David's illegitimate child as his own. But Uriah decided because his fellow soldiers were not coming home yet and the job had not been done that he was not going to go home. He was a good soldier so he slept at the door of the king's house.

This definitely complicated things a little bit. Not only had David done this horrible thing to one of his own soldiers, he did it to probably one of the best, most loyal soldiers in his army. I can only imagine how this guilt and shame must just be piling higher and higher on top of David. What David does next is truly terrible. He sends Uriah back to the field. He has Uriah hand deliver a letter to Joab who is the leader of the army. The letter told Joab to have Uriah stand on the front lines. In the heaviest, most heated part of the battle. Then have everyone else step back. Effectively he had Uriah deliver his own order of execution. Now this is a really quick overview of 2 Samuel 11. But what I really want to look at is 2 Samuel 12.

God sends a prophet named Nathan to David. Nathan tells David a story of two men. One rich, one poor. The rich man had tons of sheep and the poor man had only one. The poor man loved this sheep. This sheep grew up with him and his children. It shared his food, drank from his cup, and even slept in his arms. It was like a daughter to him. One day a traveler came to the rich man but the rich man did not want to use one of his own sheep to prepare a meal for the traveler. Instead he took the sheep from the poor man and used that to prepare the meal. Now, does this situation sound familiar at all?

Upon hearing this story David becomes enraged. The Bible actually says that David's anger burned greatly against the man and he said "As the Lord lives, surely this man who has done this deserves to die. He must make restitution for the lamb fourfold, because he did this thing and had no compassion." Nathan then turns to rebuke David, telling him that he is this man and he sinned against God by doing this. David is remorseful and repents of what he did.

I wanted to look specifically at the rebuking here. The criticism. Now this is obviously different from the criticism the Beatles received. Theirs was not from God, but it was criticism nonetheless. But Nathan was someone who had the authority to be completely open with David. David knew Nathan was speaking on behalf of God and when Nathan did speak, David made sure he listened.

I do think it is important to be open to criticism. But to a certain degree you need to be able to tune a lot of that out. This is something that I struggled with for such a long time. I am sure you have heard the phrase "If you live for people's approval, You will die for their rejection". This was definitely me. I got so worked up and worried about what everyone thought of me and my actions. And I mean EVERYONE! People that I had almost no interaction with. I would find myself staying up late at night wondering what they thought of something I did or said or didn't do or didn't say. And many times it was over the dumbest things.

I remember a specific instance, and honestly have no idea why this is still in my memory. One day when I was nine, maybe ten years old I was late getting to school. I remember I was late because I had a doctor's appointment that morning. I had those pretty frequently when I was younger because of some health issues, so this showing up late was a decently normal occurrence for me. The next thing that happened I remember in very vivid detail. Walking into the school and going into the office. Something that seems so simple, ended up being a very difficult situation for me. My mom had dropped me off at the front of the school building and then left because she had other stuff she had to attend to. In rural Illinois in the late-90's it was safe enough to just pull up to the building in the middle of the day, let your kid out, and drive away. She had already called the school and informed them I would be coming in late, so the receptionist was awaiting my arrival.

There was another student in the office when I walked in. I had never seen this student before, but I believe they were a few grades older than I was. To this day I still remember the black hooded pull over they had on. The yellow outline of a smiley face with X's for eyes and its tongue sticking out. And the word NIRVANA in all caps across the top. Even though there were three open seats in the office, this student had decided to stand up. Leaning with their back against the wall and their right foot out in front of them a little ways and their left foot kicked back resting against the wall as well. As I walked in they looked up at me, and didn't remove their stare until I had cleared the room. I was checked in and told to go ahead and go to my class. Looking back now I believe the entire exchange lasted about a minute. Maybe a little more or a little less. But for some reason, I remember **FREAKING OUT** on the inside. Like I was almost having a full scale panic attack. I was worrying about what this other student thought about me showing up to school late.

Did they think I was lazy and overslept? Maybe they thought I was faking being sick, but I was found out and sent to school. Or even worse, maybe they thought I was a bad kid and was cutting class but got caught. They had no idea that I had a doctor's appointment that morning, and was just coming back from that, and they never would know. I would never have a chance to plead my case in front of this jury of my peer. I never found out what this kid thought of me. I don't even remember ever seeing them again. But their opinion mattered to me. It mattered so extremely that it affected my physical well being for the rest of the day. I literally felt sick with worry over what this other kid thought of me.

Now I am aware this is a little bit of an extreme example, but it works nonetheless. Most were not like me and didn't struggle with crippling anxiety. But I do believe, to some extent, we all suffer or have suffered for a need of others approval.

As I stated before, this is not something that I struggle with anymore. Actually I would say I have moved much more on the opposite end of the spectrum. I should probably care a little more about what the general public thinks of me. Don't get me wrong, there isn't anything glaringly wrong with me (according to most people). I am a generally nice person. I have good hygiene. And there really isn't anything about me that would draw your interest if we were in a crowded room together. But generally speaking, I do not care what you, or most other people think of me.

I do still have people I am accountable to in different areas of my life. And there are some people whose opinions of my words and actions mean the world to me. I have given those people the permission to speak into my life to an extent that no one else has. My dad and my wife are two of the biggest ones. If either of them tell me that they have an issue with something I am doing or saying, I instantly have an issue with it as well. There are times where after evaluation I decide that I still have the same opinion, or I don't think I was wrong. There are also times where I have completely changed my stance on something based on what they had said to me. But their opinions of me play a massive role in me defining who I am.

I think this is a good thing. And I think we saw this in the story of the Beatles as well. They did take criticism and made a change to themselves. Even after they were rejected. They still saw the positive influence constructive criticism could have, especially coming from someone who is invested in your success. They were even willing to make a change to their lineup based on some criticism, that could not have been easy.

I would like to end this first chapter with my first big takeaway. Tune out everyone, except the ones you can't. I'm not saying that there are people or voices that we can't ignore. I might very well be crazy, but I'm not hearing voices. What I'm saying is that there are going to be some that we should not tune out. They are there, probably in your life already. Maybe you are like me and one is a parent, or a significant other. Maybe one is a really close friend or co-worker. Whoever it is, they will have a few defining characteristics.

Firstly, they are not afraid to hurt your feelings. The people whose opinions you take the most to heart should not be people that just tell you what you want to hear. Actually I would even go a step further and say if there is anyone in your life that is simply telling you what you want to hear, a "Yes Man" if you will, then tell them to leave. Or at the very least stop taking any significant advice from them. If they cared about you they would not be doing that. That is not beneficial to you or them, and it's probably wasting both your time and theirs. Tell them they can come back when they want to be real with you. The people whose words you should take to heart should be people who are willing to hurt your feelings for your betterment. They will be blunt with you. Possibly even to the point of making you want to curl up under your blankets and cry. But if you really think about it the criticism is usually valid. And even if you don't change your stance or your opinion you can usually take away something from what they have said.

A good example of this first one for me is with my Dad. There have been multiple times that I have tried sitting down to write something. Sometimes music lyrics, sometimes a book or story. My Dad is usually one of the first (and sometimes only) people that I ask for their opinion on my work. Even now while I'm writing this I've already gotten his feedback on the introduction. He is also going to read through the entirety of the book and give me his thoughts. I am sure I will end up making changes according to some things that he will say to me. But writing has never been something I have felt confident in. He knows that. He wants me to succeed at it. But he is also not afraid to tell me when something I've written sucks. Now he may not use those terms exactly, but he will not hesitate to point out flaws in what I have done. And there are times when it hurts. But I'm grateful. I'm grateful to have someone who cares enough to hurt my feelings.

Secondly, they are someone who wants you to succeed. They are happy for you when you do well. And they are happy for you on account of your success. They don't want to steal your thunder, and they are not jealous of you. They are even willing to sacrifice something of themselves in order to make your life better. Sometimes that sacrifice is small, sometimes it may be big, but it is costly nonetheless.

While my wife (Tiffany) and I were still just engaged we lived about an hour apart from each other. There was one day I had gone home after work. I was feeling particularly low. I really wanted to see her. My depression had dug in deep and reared its ugly head. She knew this, but she also knew I had my daughter with me, and I had to work the next day so I was not able to make the trip to go see her that night. I was just prepared to suffer through it for the night, try to get an hour or two of sleep, and get up for work the next day hoping to feel better. I decided to go to the gym with my daughter to see if that would help refocus my mind, but it didn't. I felt like I wanted to cry, and really didn't have a reason for that feeling. On a side note, depression is a real beast to fight with. Just in case you were not aware. Anyways, I got my daughter and left the gym early. I did not want to be there because I didn't want to lose control of my emotions in front of people. I went home, walked inside, and who should I find sitting on my couch? Tiffany! In the flesh. She had decided she wanted to surprise me, to help maybe bring me out of my funk. She made the hour-long trip to come see me. And on top of that she had put together a little goodie bag for me as well. Got a Chicago Cubs hat, and way more sugar free chocolate than I needed. I was doing the Keto diet at the time so sugar free was all I could have. This may not seem like much on the outside. But to me, at that moment, it was huge. It was not a huge sacrifice on her part, but it was still a sacrifice. And she willingly sacrifices on a regular basis if it benefits me.

You probably already know who these individuals are in your own life. My advice is to tell them they have permission to point out areas where you need to improve, and areas where you are already doing well. Let them know that you are wanting to grow. You are wanting to be a better person. You are wanting to learn from your failures and wanting to improve going forward. Tell them you need their help in order to do so. Ask them if they can care enough about you to hurt your feelings. Then listen to them.

Chapter 2

I Am Not Stupid!

I am not stupid! At least not anymore, and not in my own mind. I am sure there are people in this world who would probably say that statement is more objective and biased than a true statement of fact. But I've always felt I can self evaluate fairly well. And honestly if I lean towards any direction I am much more critical of myself than I am accepting. But I have said all of that to say this. I have always considered myself to be a pretty intelligent person. Now I am no Einstein, I know my limitations. But generally speaking, I think I am a fairly intelligent individual. I can grasp a wide array of decently complex topics pretty quickly. I can also communicate complicated ideas and issues in a way that is easy to understand.

You might not believe that. Or even if you do, it probably wouldn't be your first assessment if you were to look at my past. But before we get into that I want to get into another of our famous historical figures.

This is one of the stories I will tell here that may not be quite as uncommon. I mean, I believe there is no shortage of people who have heard this story, or at least some part or variation of it. The story goes that a teacher told Thomas Edison's mother that he was "too stupid to learn anything, and that he should go into a field where he might succeed by virtue of his pleasant personality". First of all, to any parents reading this. How would you like that level of brutal honesty at a parent teacher conference? Now I can't speak completely for the validity of this story in its entirety. But sources that I found were simply people stating that they had heard it, without giving much source for where they heard it from. We do know that Edison was removed from formal schooling and was instead taught by his mother. We do know that Edison was described by his teachers as addled. There is this version of the story where the teacher just flat out told Edison that he was stupid. There is another version of the story that says he brought a note home to his mother and this note had the lovely little piece of encouragement written in it, but Edison's mother couldn't bring herself to tell him so she made up a story about how he was too "gifted" or "special" to attend the school and needed to stay home for that reason.

We may never know for sure what parts of this story (if any) are true, but I for one chose to believe they are. I have heard that this is strictly an American phenomenon, but there is something truly amazing about a good underdog story. About beating the odds, achieving the impossible, and changing the world. Every young boy wants to slay the dragon and save the princess. But even if the story is not completely true there is a great deal we can learn from Thomas Edison. A shining example of what I hope to capture in this book.

For someone who seemed to come out with a new invention about as regularly as the English monarchy came out with a new tax, he had several attempts that never panned out. When asked about some of his mistakes he said some of my favorite quotes of all time "I have not failed 10,000 times, I've simply found 10,000 ways that will not work". When asked about failing to create the lightbulb 1,000 times he said "I didn't fail 1,000 times. The lightbulb was an invention with 1,000 steps". And lastly, probably my favorite quote from Thomas Edison "Many of life's failures are people who did not realize how close they were to success when they gave up". Very thought provoking statements and an extremely motivating story. You have probably never heard of most of Edison's failures, and that's probably because he never spent a lot of time looking at them.

I'm a big sports fan and I love football. It is probably my favorite sport. One thing you hear about the really great quarterbacks is that they have a short memory. You threw an interception? Ok? Get back out there next time and march your team down the field to score. Don't focus on the negative outcome you just had because you will get in your own head and you are much more likely to stay in that pattern if you do that. Thomas Edison had some pretty massive failures that probably would have derailed most other people. I know I've felt like I could not come back from some things that seem miniscule compared to some of his.

Edison made an automatic vote recorder. This was a device that allowed officials who voted on a bill to cast their votes and it would be recorded and tallied automatically. Sounds helpful doesn't it? Well many political leaders in Washington thought the opposite. They feared it would mess with the legislative process too much and he was turned away.

As many companies began to grow there was a large demand for any technology that made it easier and faster to complete administrative tasks.

Edison saw an opportunity to do this by allowing individuals to fill out multiple copies of the same form all at once. The electric pen was basically a needle, powered by a small engine and a battery. The needle moved up and down as the employee wrote. But instead of pushing out ink, the needle merely punched holes into the paper. There were many flaws with the electric pen, one of which was the noisiness while being used. Edison eventually gave up on it and sold the rights away to focus on the telephone and phonograph.

Edison had his hand in the child toy industry as well. Actually coming out with a talking doll that was put out on the market. Edison imported dolls from Germany and placed a smaller version of his phonograph inside of them. After continued production issues the dolls hit the market almost a year and a half later than Edison had originally wanted. But the dolls started coming back almost immediately. They were too fragile for young girls to play with and reportedly sounded very ghastly as well, not something most young girls would probably want to play with. Less than a month after they had originally shipped, the dolls were off of the market. This is a shining example of exactly how Edison viewed failure. You learn from it. You grow from it. And you move on. There is no reason to hold onto any of it anymore. If I am being completely honest, In researching Thomas Edison for this book I was simply floored with the number of failures he had. His attitude, from everything I have been able to find, remained really spectacular throughout. I think that probably has something to do with why most people are not really aware of these failures too. He never focused on them for too long so it was harder for others to as well. Especially when he started pumping out the ones that worked.

It took me a while to settle on a biblical figure to examine for this chapter but I think I selected one who really pairs well with the rest of the chapter. Like David in the previous chapter this is a person that I believe most people have at least a passing familiarity with, but not a deep knowledge of the backstory and how truly amazing it is. For this chapter I would like to talk about Joseph.

Now you may remember the story of the boy with the Multicolored cloak, but that is really just barely scratching the surface of the story of Joseph. His story is one of the most excellent examples of being persistent and persevering through adversity that the world has ever seen. The story of Joseph starts in Genesis 37. As I said in the previous chapter, this will be a summarization of the events that took place, but I highly encourage you to go read the story in full if you have never done so.

The story of Joseph starts off by telling us that he was the favorite of all his siblings. This caused his brothers to really really not like Joseph. I mean I kind of get it. I can relate to not being the favorite. You always get in trouble but the favorite child can do whatever and get away with it. And on top of that they get the best and first choice of everything. On a side note, Mom & Dad I'm only kidding. But not really, because Alyssa was definitely the favorite growing up. Love you both though!

Anyways, the stage was already set for Joseph's brother to really despise him. But as if it was not enough that he was the favorite he starts having dreams. In the first dream they were binding sheaves of grain in a field, when all of a sudden Joseph's sheaf stands upright and all his brothers sheaves gather around it and bow down to it. Then he had a second dream in which the Sun, Moon, and eleven stars all gathered around him bowing down to him.

As you can imagine all of his brothers were just absolutely thrilled to hear this. They actually had not had enough of Joseph being the favorite, so these constant dreams where he was very clearly positioned as being better than them came as great relief to all his brothers....I really like Sarcasm if you have not picked up on that yet. But no, these dreams made his brothers hate him even more.

Now the story skips ahead a little bit and we see Joseph's brothers are letting their father's flocks graze and Joseph is sent to go check on them. But his brothers see him coming from a distance and begin to plot to kill him. But one brother (Reuben) actually changed their minds and convinced them to throw him into a pit instead. So when he arrives they strip him down and throw him into this big pit. Then they just so happen to notice a caravan going by and decide selling him into slavery would be the best option. I mean why kill your siblings when you can just enslave them instead right? Then they slaughtered an animal, rubbed its blood on Joseph's colorful coat, took it back to their father and told him that Joseph is dead.

Jump ahead to Genesis 39 and we see that Joseph has been taken down to Egypt and sold to a man named Potiphar. Now God made Joseph prosper in everything he did, and Potiphar took notice of that. So much so that he put Joseph in charge of everything in his house. Then Potiphar's wife noticed how handsome and "well-built" Joseph was and she asked him to come to bed with her. But Joseph refused. He said that the Potiphar had entrusted him with everything in the house and it would be wrong and taking advantage of him to have relations with his wife. Then one day Joseph shows up to Potiphar's house and none of the servants were there. Then Potiphar's wife again makes a move on Joseph, but this time she grabs ahold of his cloak and tells him to come to bed with her. Not only does he decline her "invitation" he takes off. Like leaves his cloak behind and full on sprints out of the house! Now that is some dedication if I do say so myself. You would think this attitude of Joseph's would be rewarded, but we have pretty much the opposite.

Potiphar's wife calls the other servants back in and shows them Joseph's cloak. She also makes up a story saying that Joseph came onto her, trying to make her sleep with him, but she screamed so he ran away and left his cloak. Then Potiphar himself comes back and she tells him the story. The Bible says that Potiphar burned with anger towards Joseph, and had him thrown into prison with all of the King's prisoners. But as soon as Joseph was in prison we see similar circumstances. Joseph was given favor by God. Everything he does or touches he sees success in. So much so that the warden of the prison put Joseph in charge of everything in the prison. The Bible even says that the warden paid no attention to the things that were under Joseph's care.

Next we see a situation where the cupbearer and baker for the King do something wrong and both of them end up being thrown in prison under the care of Joseph. After they had been in custody for a while they both had dreams that they thought had deeper meaning, but they didn't think there was anyone around to interpret them. Little did they know the prisoner who was in charge of them would be able to tell them exactly what these dreams meant.

The cupbearer tells his dream to Joseph. In his dream there was a vine, this vine had three branches. As soon as it budded it blossomed, and its clusters ripened into grapes. Pharaoh's cup was in his hand. He took the grapes and squeezed them into the cup, then put the cup in Pharaoh's hand. Joseph was able to interpret the dream to mean that in three days Pharaoh would restore the cupbearer to his previous position. Joseph also told the cupbearer to remember him and show him kindness to get him out of prison.

Now when the baker heard this interpretation and how good it was going to be for the cupbearer he got really excited. He had a dream as well and wanted to hear the great things that Joseph would be able to interpret from his dream. But the baker would be sadly disappointed with his interpretation. He goes on to tell Joseph that in his dream there were three baskets of bread sitting on top of his head. In the top basket were all kinds of baked goods for Pharaoh, but birds were eating them out of that basket. Joseph told the baker that his dream meant that in three days Pharaoh would cut off his head, impale his body on a pole, and birds would eat his flesh. This next part is not actually in the biblical text, but I'm gonna go out on a limb and say this is not what the baker was expecting or hoping for.

Now after 3 days had passed everything came true for both the cupbearer and the baker just as Joseph had said it would happen in his interpretation. But after the cupbearer was put back in his place he forgot about Joseph. So Joseph remained in prison. Then two years later Pharaoh had need of a dream interpreter.

Pharaoh actually had two dreams. In the first he was standing by the Nile river when seven fat and healthy cows came up out of the river and began grazing around the river. Then seven ugly, very skinny cows came up behind the first seven and ate them. Then Pharaoh woke up and went back to sleep and had a second dream. In this dream seven healthy heads of grain were growing on a stalk. Then seven thin and scorched heads popped out of the stalk and they consumed the seven healthy heads and Pharaoh woke up again. Pharaoh called together all of his magicians and wisemen but none of them were able to tell him what his dream meant. Then the cupbearer remembered what had happened to him in Prison and told Pharaoh about it.

Pharaoh has Joseph brought before him and asks him to interpret the dreams. Joseph says that he can't, but God will. Then Joseph tells Pharaoh the two dreams mean the same thing. There are going to be seven years of extreme prosperity and plenty for Egypt. That will be followed by seven years of famine. God has revealed this so that they may prepare for the seven bad years during the seven good years. This ends up coming to pass just as Joseph predicts and the entire country and surrounding area is saved because of Joseph being in this position to help.

The story does go on and has a really good redemptive ending between Joseph and his brothers. But I want to focus on the lead up here. Joseph had failure after failure after failure. Sure they may not have been directly caused by his own actions, but I believe you can count these situations (at least from Joseph's perspective) as a kind of failure.

There are two main points I want to touch on with this story.

1. We never see Joseph have a bad attitude about his circumstances. Now I'm sure he had days where he was questioning what was going on, but you can very noticeably see that he keeps a strong work ethic and what seems to be a generally positive attitude throughout.
2. This is a beautiful illustration of what we see later in The Bible in Romans 8:28 "We know that God causes all things to work together for good for those who are called according to his purpose." Joseph would not have been able to save Egypt (and by extension his own family) had he not been in prison. Never would have been in prison if he was not falsely accused of try to have sex with Potapher's wife. Wouldn't have been accused if he hadn't been sold into slavery by his brothers. And so on and so on. It is a very inspiring and very reassuring chain of events to watch unfold.

Now my story isn't quite on the level of Joseph, or Thomas Edison, but I have still been able to learn from it. I did pass high school and did so pretty easily. But my grades were definitely not where they could have been. I just kind of stopped caring and got to the point that I did not do any work outside of school. If I didn't do it in class, I just didn't do it. I took a couple of assignments home with me freshman year, but that was the extent of my trying outside of the 4 walls of the school building. And actually I never took a single textbook home Sophomore, Junior, or Senior year. No work, no studying, nothing. I was cursed with a good memory and great ability of recollection. I could just remember hearing the teacher talk about the topic and I would ace most of my tests. On top of that I was also pretty good with inferring and making educated guesses. These two "skills" balanced out the missing homework that I never did.

Now I don't know where I would have ended up being if I had actually applied myself in school. I may not have finished at the top of my class. Or even in the top 5 or top 10. But I probably would have done much better than I ended up doing.

College was a little bit of a different story for me. I didn't graduate college. I failed. And more than just failed, I had 4 failed attempts at school. The first one was at a local university here in Illinois. It was close to where I grew up. I was excited to start, and I was pursuing a degree in history. If you can't tell from this book, I am pretty fond of history! But life happened. Something happened that completely altered my course in life. I became a dad. My daughter was born literally the day before I started my first semester. I still went to school, and worked full time on top of that to support my family. But I couldn't keep up. I wasn't good enough. Now please don't misinterpret what I am saying here. I wouldn't change anything about this, because I have grown quite fond of my oldest daughter. Even though she now has decided to grow this attitude out of nowhere and has the quick wit of her father to boot. I must say I am still a pretty big fan. But I wasn't good enough to complete school while working a full time job. I know so many people that have done this and I have a deep level of respect for them. My dad is one. He worked a full time job and went to school full time and still made time for our family and made the National Dean's list a couple of times as well. But I couldn't do it. My grades started to slip, because I was having to miss classes. Then I made the decision to quit. But honestly, I was quitting to avoid failing. But looking back now I still consider it to be failing, even if it wasn't "official".

My next endeavor at higher education was with an online school. Let me preface this by saying online schooling is not for the lazy. You must be extremely self driven and determined in order to succeed in it. This was something that I did not realize and did not take into consideration when I started. At the time I was not self driven or very determined. I was tired of working physically exhausting and demanding jobs. I wanted to be able to get a job that I would enjoy, I would make more money doing, and that wouldn't kill me physically. But I wasn't determined enough. The online school I started attending was set up so that you could graduate at a much faster rate, but it also required you to complete more school work and classes in a much shorter amount of time. I was not prepared, and it didn't take long for me to start falling behind. Once again I made the decision to drop out before I could actually fail. And once again, in my eyes that is still a failure.

My third attempt started off much better. It was another online school, but I was prepared this time. I was doing really well. Even made the National Dean's list. Finally I was getting it. Then, once again, life decided to throw a curveball. I started having issues in my marriage. Now I'll go more into detail about this in a later chapter, but for time restraints I will have to sum it up here. I couldn't focus on my schooling because my focus was on the fact that my marriage was falling apart. And when that started to happen it didn't take long for my grades to start reflecting it. But this time, I was determined not to quit. I pushed and persevered. I worked my butt off every single day. Even times when I had to finish homework assignments while cooking dinner for three kids and making sure my clothes were ready for work for the next day. And then it finally happened. All of my hard work finally paid off. I graduated!!! Just kidding, I failed again. And this time I actually tried to stick it out, so I can't even say that I quit to avoid failing. I didn't know what to do, so I stopped trying. For a very long time.

My last attempt at college was probably the most defeating to me mentally. Mainly because it was the one that felt the most out of my control. Once again I tried my hand at online school. And once again I was prepared for the challenges that I would face in attending. I made spreadsheets that I used to track my assignments. Both my due dates and my grades. I'm kind of a spreadsheet nerd so I made these actually factor up my grades automatically based on the point value of each assignment. It also showed me what my grade would be at any given point if I failed out based on the grades I had already received. I had these available to me all day, everyday. I set up reminders every day to get onto my classes and do something. Even if I didn't have an assignment to work on. I would get on and review the material for that week, or look ahead at the material for the next week. I was nothing if not determined to finish and get my degree. I was tired of being a failure. And this time I was finally going to do something about it.

Four classes in and I was going strong. I was blocking out distractions, I was sticking to my plans to complete assignments and I was getting A's on every assignment in every class. It was working. Then I received a call from the school. I couldn't sign up for my next class because I had reached my maximum amount allowed to borrow for student aid. I applied for several other grants and scholarships, but it was all for nothing. I had finally gotten to the point where I was doing it. I was passing. More than just passing, I was excelling in my schooling. But my past failures came back to rear their ugly head one last time.

I struggled for so long with this. I always felt like less than. Like a second class citizen, because I wasn't able to complete college. I don't hold this view of others that are in the same situation though. As I said at the beginning of this chapter, I am a much bigger critic of myself than anyone else is. But I'm also more forgiving and understanding of others going through the same situation as I am.

I am not sure exactly where or why I became this way, but I picked it up somewhere. And no matter how hard I have tried I can't shake it. I can however remain aware of that downfall. This is where Chapter one comes into play. The aforementioned individuals. My Dad and Tiffany. Not only do they tell me I am wrong when I need to hear it, but they tell me I'm right when I need it too. There have been plenty of times where I have doubted myself, or something I have done. They are quick to build me up. And not just generic "oh that's good". But they can pull specifics from things I've done or said and show me why it is good. One reason I can value their praise so much is because that's not all they do. I mentioned in the previous chapter that they care enough about me to hurt my feelings. Because of that, I know their praise isn't hollow. They are never going to simply tell me what I want to hear, or tell me something is good when it is not. The praise is genuine, because the criticism is as well.

Chapter 3

<u>Stop Never Stopping</u>

This chapter almost looked very different. I have always had the same biblical story and story from my personal life, but I originally had a completely different first story for this chapter. Not that my previous selection was not good, I had just originally overlooked who I decided to write this on. You see, with my current job I have a lot of monotonous work. Very repetitive stuff where I don't need to think a lot. This allows me to listen to a lot of different stuff while I am working. Occasionally I will listen to music, but normally I listen to talking. Lectures, podcasts, teaching, preaching, really anything where I can learn something while I am working. That led me to a video about a man that I thought I knew a decent amount about, but I did not realize how much of his story I was missing out on. And how perfectly his story ties into what I am discussing in this chapter.

Elon Musk has been really capturing a lot of attention recently. From sending a rocket into space, to buying Twitter and claiming he wants to turn the physical building headquarters into a homeless shelter (I completely believe this is something he would do and would be a great idea) Musk seems to be making headlines pretty much every single day. I have always really had a pretty decent opinion of Elon Musk, admittedly I do not know him personally. And I do not think I probably ever will although I would love the opportunity to meet him. But from what I can see of him he is a very open, honest, and humble person. And those are three qualities that I find to be extremely rare, and of utmost importance.

So I stumbled across a video titled something like "If you don't like Elon Musk watch this video" and it sounded interesting to me so I decided to listen to it while I worked. As the video played I found myself just stopping working in order to watch him in these interviews. The insight he has is amazing and his story is truly remarkable.

I think most people know that Musk was born and raised early on in South Africa. Jump ahead to college age and you will find him at the University of Pennsylvania. Where he earned a bachelors in economics and in physics. He also financed his own way through college. After this he started a PhD program at Stanford but dropped out early on to pursue his entrepreneurial dreams.

He helped found a company called Zip2 that struggled financially for a while before it took off. But Musk was determined. I heard him in an interview describing how he and his brother (his brother worked with him on this startup) could not afford a place to live so they just slept on a couch in the office of their startup. He would also use a local YMCA to shower. Eventually Zip2 did take off and would sell for $307 million in 1999. Musk's share of that was $22 million.

Musk turned around and put these earnings into his next project. He helped start X.com, one of the first online banks. In 2000 X.com merged with another company and the new merged company changed its name to PayPal. PayPal was purchased by Ebay in 2002 for $1.5 billion. Normally you could expect someone who made this much money on one event to retire early. But not Musk. In the interviews I listened to I heard him describe sitting on a beach doing nothing as torture. He could do it for a little while, but not for a sustained amount of time. I can definitely relate to that. The thought of just sitting and doing nothing drives me crazy.

Musk had received $180 million from the buyout of PayPal. Of that $180 million he said the following "My proceeds for the PayPal acquisition were $180 million. I put $100 million in SpaceX, $70 million in Tesla. I had to borrow money for rent."

Tesla was founded in 2003 by Musk and a couple of other individuals. In 2004 he made a $6.5 million investment and became the largest shareholder of the company. In 2008 he became the company's CEO, and in 2009 they would begin production on its first car model. I actually remember when the Tesla Roadster came out. I was very surprised to see how completely stunning it looked. Now I did not think that Tesla was going to put out an ugly car by any means, but I still remember being very pleasantly surprised when I saw them for the first time.

Around this time Musk also founded aerospace company SpaceX. I have heard him say in several different interviews that he wants to make space travel available and affordable to virtually everyone. This is an incredible endeavor and is something I never thought I would see in my lifetime. In 2010 SpaceX became the first commercial company to ever send a spacecraft into orbit and return it safely. This was not their first time trying though. This was actually their fourth attempt to put a spacecraft into orbit and have it return successfully. At this point SpaceX was almost out of money. According to Musk they were virtually running on fumes. He wanted to get the best people in to work on the project, but was somewhat unsuccessful in some spots. As chief engineer he said none of the good engineers wanted to do the job, and the bad engineers that did, well why would you want a bad chief engineer. So Musk ultimately became the chief engineer himself.

Now if you look forward 11 years SpaceX completed its first orbital launch of an all-private crew. Meanwhile at the beginning of 2022 it was estimated that Tesla had 2 vehicles (Model Y & Model 3) that were in the top 20 in the U.S. in vehicle sales. Pretty impressive if I do say so myself... and I do.

Now it was not always just success after success for Musk. There was actually a point where the United States had a bad recession in 2008 called "The Great Recession". In interviews I have heard Musk talk about how Tesla was weeks away from being dead in the water. Single digit weeks. That would be a scary thought as a founder and CEO. Not only have you poured all this money into it, but your time and life as well.

There were a couple of things I heard him say over and over that I really wanted to hit on in this chapter. The first is about fear. In talking about both companies almost going under he said "drive overrides fear. But I feel the fear. It's kind of annoying, I wish I didn't, I wish I felt it less." Fear is something we all struggle with, but most people do not want to admit it. Most people try to just act like they are not afraid. The "Fake it til you make it" mentality. But what I have seen from Musk is a much different attitude. A "No I have fear, it is real, I will acknowledge it. But the stakes are too high for me to be crippled by it so I am going to keep pushing forward". I would like to reiterate the three qualities I mentioned previously. Open, honest, and humble. You can identify all three in this attitude and I believe it has contributed greatly to his success.

The second thing I heard him say is probably my favorite. It is very against what is pushed in our culture today. "Sometimes don't give up, is really bad advice". He used the example of someone using their head to break through a brick wall. Obviously in this situation it would be hateful to tell the person not to give up. It is kind, loving and important to tell people to stop doing something if they are doing something that is detrimental to their mental, physical, or spiritual well being. I would say Elon Musk is well known for being blunt and to the point, which I absolutely love! I am very much the same way. Sometimes it is a good trait, sometimes it is not the best way to handle a situation. But it is my default and I love seeing it. I think good evidence of this can be found in his twitter thread.

One tweet says "The attacks against me should be viewed through a political lens - this is their standard (despicable) playbook - but nothing will deter me from fighting for a good future and your right to free speech".

The next tweet was a retweet of a previous tweet of his from 3/25/21. The original tweet said "If there's ever a scandal about me, *please* call it Elongate". The retweet said "Finally, we get to use Elongate as scandal name. It's kinda perfect." In short I really like Elon Musk, and I think if more people had his drive and attitude the world would be a better place.

Now if I have not given some of you a reason to hate me yet, please allow me to correct that. I am a Patriots fan. Yes even now that Tom Brady is "Tampa Brady" I am still a New England loyal. But what I have seen from Musk has honestly reminded me a good bit of Brady. Simply put, I would never bet against Brady. Now I might end up on the losing side of some bets, but more often than not I will win. Why? Because I know every time he walks onto the field he has worked harder than anyone else in the building. Going forward I am going to have the same philosophy with Musk. I do not know what all endeavors he will venture into in the future, but I am betting on Elon. Despite whatever the situation may look like. Simply because I know no one is going to out work him! And that accounts for a lot.

The biblical story I want to tell for this section starts in Genesis 29. The actual storyline starts a little ways before that but I will summarize it. Jacob was the son of Isaac, brother of Esau. Esau and Jacob were twins, but Esau was the first born, which entitled him to more than Jacob. But through some trickery and deceit Jacob actually takes Esau's inheritance or blessing from him. Esau finds out before their father Isaac dies and says when the time is over for mourning their father he is going to kill Jacob. Once Jacob finds out about this he decides it is probably best for him to head out, so he does.

This is where we find Jacob. He has come to a distant land, to the home of a man named Laban. Laban had two daughters and Jacob instantly fell completely head over heels in love with the youngest daughter. The oldest daughter was Leah and the younger daughter was Rachel (you will need to know that in just a minute). Jacob and Laban had been discussing Jacob working for him and trying to figure out what the payment would be, when Jacob said he would work for Laban for seven years to be able to marry Rachel. Talk about some dedication. And he actually had to work the full seven years before he was able to marry her. But The Bible says that the seven years seemed like only a few days for Jacob because he was so in love with Rachel.

I know this may sound a bit far fetched, but I have to say I can relate. And I think most other people could as well if they really think about it. So when my wife and I were just dating we lived just over an hour apart. We usually only got to see each other once, maybe twice a week. That hour drive to see her seemed so short. But the hour drive home seemed so much longer. Now that we're married I have about a 45 min drive one way to work. It is on the same stretch of road. And it has the same effect. My drive to work in the mornings is much longer than my drive home in the evenings. But the drive home is not just taking me home, it is leading to her.

So for seven years he worked and toiled knowing it would be worth it because he was going to get this woman that he loved so dearly. When the day finally came and his seven years was complete he went to Laban and told him "Give me my wife, for my time is completed, that I may go in to her." I know what you are thinking, you don't even need to say it. Jacob was quite the romantic! Such a way with words! But remember that during this time, one of the most important things to do was to have kids. They helped to do work that needed to be done, but also carried on your name for another generation.

Now after Jacob speaks this little love poem something very... peculiar happens. Laban brings his daughter to Jacob. Now again, I know what you're thinking. "How is that Peculiar? He is doing what he agreed to do." Well not entirely. Laban did bring his daughter to Jacob, but it was not Rachael. Remember at the beginning it specifically called out two of Laban's daughters, Leah and Rachael. Now I do not know entirely how this happened and The Bible doesn't get into the specifics of how Laban was able to trick Jacob, but I think there were a couple of things at work. Keep in mind the following points are simply my opinion. I think Laban brought Leah to Jacob when it was dark, and no electricity means it wasn't all that bright. Plus if Jacob had been working seven years for this I think he was probably just ready to receive his earnings. There also may have been some kind of veil or something covering Leah when she was brought to Jacob. Modesty was a very big part of society and I could see that being the case. But enough of my opinions, let's get back to the reading.

We pick back up in Genesis 29:25. Maybe it is just me, but I happen to find how this is written to be rather funny, so I am going to quote it directly. "So it came about in the morning that, behold, it was Leah!" Behold is defined as "to see or observe (a thing or person, especially a remarkable or impressive one)". Maybe it is just me but I picture this being a very hilarious interaction taking place the morning after, I also feel pretty bad for Leah, but I have to think she was at least somewhat in on this whole thing. Like I really cannot believe she had no idea that the wool (or goatskin) was being pulled over Jacob's eye's (I do not care who you are, that joke was funny. If you don't get it go back and read Genesis 27). Anyways back to the story. Jacob went to Laban asking why he fooled him and Laban said basically it was not his people's custom to marry the younger daughter before the older. So basically was saying he had to, but this is also a jab flying directly in Jacob's face for what he just did to his brother (Go back and read Genesis 25 through 27). Then Laban told Jacob to spend the wedding week with Leah and then he could get Rachael as well, but he would have to work an additional seven years after receiving her as a wife. So Jacob spent the wedding week with Leah, then received Rachael as a wife as well, then worked another seven years for Laban.

Now I believe wholeheartedly that there is something admirable about being persistent. When the cards are stacked against you, or the situation is difficult in some way. Having the ability to stand up under the pressure, not flinch, and just continue to push forward is a very good trait to have. But I believe (as we saw with Musk) it is also good to know when to quit. I believe this next story from my personal life displays both of these fairly well.

I have always been the type of person that does not quit easily. But that comes in even more so when I look at my job history. I have stuck it out at difficult, overly stressful, underlie compensated jobs for far longer than I should have. But of all the times in my past that would fit this, there is one that really stands out above the others.

I worked at a third party billing company. This was in the medical field, for a specialty type of doctor. Essentially to sum it all up in a nutshell, it is very complex and complicated for doctors to bill insurance companies. Insurance companies make it like this on purpose in order to avoid paying out as much money as they can. Honestly the more you learn about the whole process the more sketchy it seems and the more it looks like the whole process needs an overhaul. But I started for this company in a department that filed claims electronically to insurance companies.

After working there for about 7 months a position opened up for the lead of the department I was in. I applied for it, and I got the job. Now I can admit that part of the reason I got the job was from a lack of interest from most other people. But part of it was due to my previous experiences and the skill set I had demonstrated already in this position. I was excited to take on the job, but things quickly started to change for me with this company.

The position above me was vacant and had been for about two months previously. Above that was actually the owner of the company as well as two other managers. The owner of the company was also a practicing doctor. Let's call him Dr. A. Dr. A also preached about not being afraid to fail, however when it came time to encourage people after the failure he was not good to follow up. But that is not the first place I started having issues.

Shortly after I was promoted to being over that one department I had another department added to me "temporarily". Then there was another department who had a lead that was… honestly just terrible at their job. Lazy, played favorites ALL the time, just not a good lead. But the decision was made to step her down from her position and put me over that department "temporarily" as well. Then there was another department that had their lead just quit. Out of nowhere with no notice. So I was thrown into that department simply to help try and figure it out while they looked for a replacement. Several weeks passed and I was still running that department as well as every other department in the company. So without any pay increase or recognition I had effectively become the operations manager. That was the vacant position I had mentioned.

HOW TO FAIL AT PRACTICALLY EVERYTHING: A COMPREHENSIVE GUIDE

Once this had started I was one of the four managers running the company. There was me, who was over the day to day of the company, A lady over HR, a guy over sales (he was also the only salesman for the company), and Dr. A. Things went on like this for a while, all while having some issues with the sales manager and Dr. A, but there are frankly too many issues to cover them all so I will just hit a few. Things did come to a head a couple times between myself and the sales manager. He wanted to receive his commission but not do the job fully, so many times doctors who were curious about our service were passed on to me. I had to answer questions about what we could do the the doctors, what we would charge, any discounts we provided, all kinds of typical questions a salesman would take in the beginning process of starting services. But they were all being pushed to me. I typed out some bullet point issues I was wanting to address. I was going to bring them to Dr. A. But before I got the chance something happened. Maybe you heard about it, but I would not be entirely surprised if you had not. It was called Covid, we had this whole global pandemic thing. I am not sure about other places, but when things started moving in Illinois they really started moving quickly. One day everything was normal, then literally the next day everyone had to stay home except "essential employees". I ended up being one of those essential employee's but the sales manager was not.

Over the course of our lockdown I did have the opportunity to talk with Dr. A about the issues I was having with the sales manager. He never really said much about it, just that he would have a discussion with the sales manager when everyone came back to work. But when that time came, the sales manager refused to return because he was getting so much more staying at home. So after this happened the sales responsibility was added onto me as well.

Next was the HR manager. After Covid hit she did come back for a short period of time. She wanted to come back, but Dr. A thought she was being paid too much money. So he tried to present an idea to her. She could come back, but it would be at a reduced salary. She decided she couldn't do that so she didn't come back. And guess what happened next? Yep, that is right! The HR responsibilities were added onto me as well. Now with these I will say that some of these responsibilities were added to a trainer we had too so it was not solely on me. But it was yet another increase in workload without an increase in compensation of any kind.

So things had gotten to be a bit much for me. The stress of all the additional workload had been really adding up on me. Plus the additional responsibilities meant I had to do a lot of work outside my clocked in hours (I was still hourly). The commission I was getting from sales was a fraction of what the previous sales manager had been paid. And to top everything off I was not allowed to make bonuses anymore because Dr. A was expecting things to be very tight financially because of Covid.

I know a lot of this seems to be coming back to money. Now with this story there is a lot of that. That is not my primary driving force, but when talking about a job or employment in general it is difficult not to put a focus on it. Especially with the nature of what I am discussing.

Everything really came to a head one day when I found out some information. I always really struggled with the idea that I had all this extra added onto me and Dr. A was honestly saving a ton of money because he had me doing the jobs of about six people, while still not making as much as the highest paid of those six people. But I really never pushed because he always made the comment that he was not taking a salary. And I occasionally saw the payroll and he was listed as an employee, but he was not taking a salary. So I guess in a way that made it easier for me to tolerate because the guy that owned the company was having to make sacrifices too. But I made some discoveries that really changed my mind permanently for the company and Dr. A and I think they sealed my fate of leaving.

The first thing I found out was Dr. A maybe was not taking a salary, but he was still making a decent amount of money from the company. See he owned the building, and the company I worked for (which he also owned) was paying him rent. Not to get into details, but he was making over three times more from that rent every month than I was making and I was running everything from the top down. Not to mention the other tenants he had in the building that were paying him rent as well.

Shortly after this I found out he was actually paying his wife and two of his kids as well. They were doing work for the company, but it was part time at best and they were making a very considerable amount of money from their very few hours.

Normally I really would not care. I think if someone owns a business, generally they should be allowed to do what they want with the resources of the business. I am very much a free market capitalist. But the beauty of free market capitalism is, if I do not like what a company is doing with their resources I am free to leave. I am not a slave or an endentourd servant. And that is something that businesses and business owners need to keep in mind. Keep employees happy, within reason, and they will stay.

The next issue tied in to the previous. When covid hit one thing we did to save money was to cut my bonuses temporarily. After things started looking better and money was coming in regularly I brought up getting my bonuses again, or atleast a bonus again, even if it wasn't what it was before.

In order to understand what happened next I need to explain something. My bonuses were tied directly to how profitable the different departments were. Not by comparison to previous months or years, but based on the average amount each employee brought in. We had it figured up so we knew what was needed to cover the cost in each department for how many employees each department had. So the more they did the more of a bonus I got. And the more they did the more of a bonus they got.

So I brought up getting bonuses again, but I was told we weren't profitable enough yet to justify any bonuses. I was told it would be better for me to not focus on bonuses because I would not be getting them right now anyway. Just focus on helping everyone be profitable in the future. I decided to look back and figure up my bonuses for the previous year. I should have made over ten thousand in bonuses. Because even despite covid we had one of our most profitable years in company history. And we did it with fewer employees too. That led to me supposed to have been getting very sizable bonuses every quarter. When I brought this to the attention of Dr. A he changed what he was saying. Now it was not that I would not get a bonus, it was that I agreed to not get bonuses anymore going forward permanently. I think it goes without saying that this really does not make sense, except to try and save money for Dr. A.

I decided to make one more attempt to make things better. I decided what it would take for me to continue working there, typed up an email to Dr. A, and sent it to him. I outlined all the additional jobs I had been given over the course of 3 years without a single increase in compensation. He responded saying he would like to talk about it in person. So we did. And I was scalded, had my job threatened, was talked down to and belittled for three and a half hours. Then he told me he would approve what I asked for.

But with all that being said it was still a difficult decision for me to make. I do not like to quit and I do not like leaving jobs. I take pride in staying at the same company for a long period of time, but I had to quit. I really did not feel like I had much of a choice in the matter. Obviously yes I could have stayed, but that job was in no way beneficial for me. So not quitting would have been horrible advice.

So I did exactly what the free market allows. I started applying for any job that I could make work. Absolutely everything, and I am incredibly thankful and happy I got the job that I did. I really could not have asked for a better job. It took me a little while, but after I left I eventually realized this was not a failure, on the contrary it was a success.

Chapter 4

Fall Six Times, Get Up Seven

So I feel like up to this point I have been pretty uncontroversial in pretty much everything I have said. Most everything I have written has been either historical fact, factual experiences of mine, with some of my opinions mixed in to add a little flavor. But nothing too "spicy". Nothing that would make anyone put down the book with disgust because they disagree on something so strongly. Something so fundamental that cuts away at the very core of their being. But I'm about to make such a statement. You're either going to agree with me completely, or disagree completely. There will be very few (if any) people in between. But here it goes. Holding nothing back... Iron Man was the best Avenger.

Now you can either agree with me or be wrong. This has even caused some tears in my family. My oldest son who is a **HUGE** fan of all things marvel disagrees with me fundamentally on this. He thinks Spiderman holds that coveted #1 spot. But alas, he is gravely mistaken. Don't worry though. I haven't kicked him out of the house just yet for holding such a farcical opinion. And he does have Tony Stark as the second best, so I hold out hope that one day we will see a conversion.

My first introduction to Robert Downey Jr. actually was not from Iron Man, that was my second real time seeing him. My first introduction was Zodiac and after that Tropic Thunder (which I must say was absolutely hilarious) but that is definitely not what launched him into fame. The son of director and actress, Downey Jr. received his first acting gig at the age of five. Shortly after, at the age of six, he was introduced to drugs by his father. Marijuana and coke were commonplace around his father and Jr. was allowed to partake in these as a way for him and his father to bond. I have a bit of a soft spot in my heart for people who struggle with addiction. I will dive a little more into the reason why later on in this chapter. But my heart goes out even more so for people who were thrust into that battle at extremely young, vulnerable, and impressionable ages.

Now before I go any further I want to say that I am not suggesting that Robert Downey Jr. should be viewed as a victim in this situation. I do not think he should be and I say that because I do not think he would want to be viewed that way. Granted I have never met, and probably never will meet RDJ, although he is one I would love to have a good conversation with, what I gather from his personality that I have seen is that he would not want to be perceived as a victim of his circumstances. Just like so many others that I know who have fought this fight and won. They are not victims of what happened, but fighters that beat it. They are overcomers, underdogs that kept getting up after every hit knocked them down.

After this RDJ would go on to have some minor roles in his fathers films. But in 1987 he landed the role that really launched his career. Playing a drug addict in the movie less than zero. From 1996 through 2001 RDJ was arrested several times on charges related to drugs and did a few unsuccessful stints in drug rehab programs. He even explained his relapses to a judge with the following "It's like I have a shotgun in my mouth, and I've got my finger on the trigger, and I like the taste of gunmetal." During his time in jail he was attacked by fellow inmates and left in a pool of his own blood.

Then in 2003 he was finally able to quit for good. He threw his drugs into the ocean after meeting Susan Levin (his current wife). And he never went back. From there he started appearing in different smaller roles (ie. Zodiac & Tropic Thunder) but then he got the opportunity of a lifetime and he capitalized on it. There is not a single person on the face of the earth that could have played the role of Tony Stark more perfectly than Robert Downey Jr. did. The Billionaire, Playboy, Philanthropist had as much whit as he had intelligence and there was no one he was afraid to go toe to toe with. By the way, that is why Tony is the only Avenger that Thanos was really afraid of.

None of the success that Downey ended up achieving was just given to him. He had to work and work and work. Had to fight hard and dig deep to get every opportunity that he received. Then when he got them he capitalized on them. I love the story of RDJ because it is a story of overcoming that stretches from "Less than Zero" to the greatest American Hero.

Now as we move on to the biblical story here I want to do something slightly different than I have done in the previous chapter. I actually want to look at two stories. The first I will touch on briefly just to illustrate a point, but the second I will go into much more detail on.

For the first story we will go back to Genesis. Specifically Genesis chapter 13. To really crudely paraphrase what is going on, Abram (Abraham before God changed his name) and Lot are leaving the land they are currently in, but they both have a lot of stuff and they decide they need to split up and go different ways. Abram told Lot to pick whatever direction he wanted to go and Abram would go the opposite direction. Let's start in verse 10.

"^{10} Lot lifted up his eyes and saw all the Valley of the Jordan, that it was well watered everywhere - this was before the Lord destroyed Sodom and Gomorrah - like the garden of the Lord, like the land of Egypt as you go to Zoar. ^{11} So Lot chose for himself all the valley of the Jordan, and Lot journeyed eastward."

There are a few points I want to bring to your attention in this story that tie into the overall theme of this chapter.

1. Lot chose what looked good to his eyes and took nothing else into consideration. Actually strike that, he may have taken one other thing into consideration. In the next chapter it says Lot settled in the cities of the valley and moved his tents as far as Sodom. That brings up the next point.
2. Lot wanted to get as close to Sodom as he could without living inside it. Now if you read on into this story you will see that Sodom could have been renamed Sin City and it would have been a much more accurate and fitting name for them than it is for Las Vegas. I am not going to expound on this point too much but I did want to touch on it. I believe this is one of the biggest issues in the church and with Christians today. Trying to get as close to sin without "technically" stepping over the line. But we are called to be set apart. To be visibly different. That does not look like getting as close as possible without stepping over. And we see this does not work out well for Lot. In the next chapter it mentions that he and everyone with him is taken captive because they are in Sodom during a time of war.
3. The last point I want to draw from this right now is the underlined

portion. Lot chose this for himself. And this is the last time we really see Lot make an active decision for himself. After this he is doing nothing more than reacting to his surroundings and what is happening to him.

I believe this is an important lesson for everyone to learn, regardless of if you are a christian or not. If you play footsie with sin, you will end up falling in. You will not even realize that it has happened until you are a prisoner of your own desires.

The next story I want to look at has very much similar themes throughout it. And although he is most famous for his association with the name Delilah, he was never formally a member of the Plain Whit T's.... at least not that I am aware of. No, I think it is safe to assume that Samson probably never picked up a guitar or microphone in his lifetime. He did do plenty of other noteworthy things though. Most people have heard of Samson, but most people also don't know his whole story. Something about strength, a girl named Delilah, somebody's hair. Did Delilah have super strong hair that she would let down out of a tower for Samson to climb up? No...wait...wrong story. This story actually happened. And is much better than any princess story. Some see it as a bad story, but I don't. see it as a story of bad decisions, leading to betrayal, which leads to defeat. The kind that you cannot come back from on your own. But through that God still shows up. Samson's story should have been over, but God had other plans.

You can read Samson's entire story in Judges chapters 13 through 16. And I really think it is worth reading to get the entire backstory of Samson. But to summarize Samson was set apart from birth. He had special rules to follow and as long as he did God's spirit was with him and gave him some incredible strength. Now throughout Samson's story he is breaking these rules. He really does not care, and he has a bit of a problem with the ladies.

This all culminates when Samson becomes involved with Delilah, who is looking to betray Samson for her people (the philistines). She wants to learn the secret of his strength (his hair) so she asks, and he tells her that if he is bound with seven fresh cords that have not been dried then he will become weak. She gets Samson to go to sleep, binds him with the cords, then yells "Samson the Philistines are upon you", but he jumps up and snaps the cords effortlessly.

Now I know what you are thinking. Wouldn't it be a little fishy that this took place? And while the answer is yes, Samson is not in his right mind. He has seen something he desires with his eyes, just like Lot previously, and he is not taking anything else into consideration. Now Delilah complains that Samson lied to her (really?) and this whole thing happens again, but Samson says he must be bound tightly with new ropes that have not been used. Delilah gets him to sleep, binds him, "Samson, the Philistines!", and boom he is up again and snapped the ropes.

Delilah complains that Samson lied to her yet again, so this time he tells her another story, but I want you to notice something. This time he is still not honest, but he is tiptoeing closer to that line. He says if she braids this fabric into his hair and tightens it with a pin he will become weak. She does this, she yells, Samson jumps up still strong. She complains again and this time he finally tells her. If his hair is cut, his strength will leave him.

Now she finally has the real source, and Sampson ends up being taken captive by the Philistines, they gouge out his eyes and use him for labor and entertainment. When Samson awoke this final time he did not even realize that God's presence had left him.

I know this sounds really depressing, and that would probably be because it is. But one of my favorite verses in this story is Judges 16:22 "but the hair on his head began to grow again" Samson ends up at the center of the temple, by the pillars that support the whole temple and he gets his strength back. Pushes those pillars out and kills more philistines in his death than he ever did in his life.

I have heard many people talk about the story of Samson as the story of a man who messed up royally... and that's it. To provide a little more context, Samson was a Judge. But not like powdered wig and black robes. Judges for Israel were the leaders of the day. Other countries had Kings or Pharaohs, but Israel had Judges and Prophets. Samson was called to lead the nation, but failed time and time again. But I do not see his story that way.

I mean yes Samson did mess up in a huge way. Quite literally did everything he was not supposed to do. But despite it all this was a story of success through redemption by the grace of God.

I tend to see myself a lot in the story of Samson. Especially the part where Delilah was very very clearly not good for him, but he just continued to be ignorant to that fact. I see myself in the story because this was me for quite a while.

I had entered into a relationship, not of my own choosing, when I was very young. It took me a long time to realize that this relationship was harmful for me. More than just harmful, it was deadly. This foul, nasty, mistress was in a very literal sense killing me from the inside out. But once I finally realized how horrible this relationship was for me it was too late. Just like Lot who I mentioned before, I was a prisoner to my own desires.

I do want to preface before I go much further, that any names, and some locations have been changed for the remainder of this chapter. This is a pretty sensitive topic, but I am not changing things for my own benefit. I am pretty open, honest, and transparent about most of my life, but especially this topic. The reason for the changing names is that this story, like almost every story, involves other people. And this may come as a shock to you, but sometimes people do really horrible and stupid things to other people. But despite that and despite how some of the decisions made by others impacted my life severely for the negative I am willing to acknowledge two things.

1. The things I went through in the past have completely shaped who I am today. And as bad as some of those things may have been, they have given me the ability to help others.
2. People are just flawed in general. And flawed people make bad decisions. There is a whole plethora of things that happen on a daily basis in our world that are horrible atrocities, worse than I have ever experienced, but they are a result of living in a fallen world.

So with those out of the way, let's dive back into the story.

My first introduction to pornography was around the age of 9. Now that is a relative guess on my age. I know I was in the ballpark of 9 years old, but I don't remember for sure. I was actually at someone else's house. I was actually somewhat lucky to have a father that had seen this battle and already started fighting it. So there was no porn in my house. Anyways, I was at the house of someone my family trusted, and was watching Willy Wonka & the chocolate factory. The one with Gene Wilder. Now this a few years ago, back in the 1999 - 2000 ballpark. So I was watching this movie on a VHS tape. Suddenly the movie cut out, and where there was once an innocent childrens movie, now was showing anything but that.

    I did not watch for long. If I am being totally honest I was incredibly embarrassed by what I had seen. I felt like I did something wrong, but I could not really say what it was. Then as the next couple of days came and went I found myself thinking more about what I had seen. Time would pass, and I would (for the most part) forget about what I had seen. But there had been a change in me from that moment. Even with it being a very short exposure it affected me. I had a sister who played a lot with barbie dolls. I started noticing that the adult female barbies had much larger chests than the ken dolls or even the younger girl dolls. And I noticed that I started realizing these different things, but it all just festered inside of me. I did not hear or see anyone else talking about any of this and I felt like this was something I was the only one who knew anything about.

    This curiosity continued in me until I was 13 years old. I remember moving to a new school and making new friends. If I am being honest I really did not like my new school that much. Or my new friends really for that matter. But they were friends none the less so I still tried to hang out with and talk to them.

    I remember I was really into this one online game. It was kind of like a virtual chat room type thing. They were pretty big in the early 2000's. But in this one you got to make your own avatar and had your own apartment thing. You could even get custom furniture and stuff for it. I was talking with one of my friends about it one day when we were at my house after school. My parents were both working and my sister was somewhere else. So my friend and I were alone. I remember him telling me he had another really cool site that he thought I would like. So he took over on the computer, typed in the web address, hit enter, and my world was changed forever.

    Images and videos lit up my computer monitor, the likes of which I had never seen before. Shortly after that it was time for my friend to go, but the damage had been done. I had full trust from my parents, I mean as far as they knew I was not even aware this stuff existed. But now I did. And even more than that, I had a computer in my room on the second floor of our house with every other bedroom on the bottom floor.

For the next two years I fed, increased, and expanded my appetite for this garbage. Completely and totally unrestrained. My parents did not find out I was looking at anything until I was 15 years old. But even when they found out I was able to quickly hide it. Because they had no idea I had been looking consistently for two years already. This was a simple accident, so I just got more careful and we moved on as if I was not addicted to it.

When I turned 16 I got my first smartphone. This was the worst thing to ever happen to my sexual, mental, physical, and spiritual well being. This catapulted me into a life of perversion that if not for the grace of God I would not be here today.

How pornography works is it allows you to slowly kill yourself. I have a little story as an illustration. It's an instructional story of how an eskimo kills a wolf. Now, I do want to preface this story as well. I have heard it in several different places from several different people. I cannot say for certain this is an accurate depiction of the process an eskimo would have taken to kill a wolf. I can say however it is a completely accurate description of how an addiction to porn looks.

The story goes that to kill a wolf an eskimo will first take an extremely sharp knife and dip it in blood. He will allow that blood to freeze, then dip it in blood again. He will repeat this process until there are multiple layers of frozen blood on this knife. He will then dip it in fresh blood one last time and stick it in the ground blade up. The wolf (with his keen sense of smell) picks up on the blood, tracks it down, and begins licking it off of the blade. He continues to do this until he eventually cuts his tongue and/ or mouth on the knife. Before long he is licking his own blood and not even realizing it. The eskimo will return the next day to find the wolf lying dead next to the knife.

I would like to reiterate, I am not an eskimo. Or an expert on eskimo hunting traditions and practices. But I have gone through this addiction first hand. Just like the wolf in the story, it was pure lust that led me to that knife. I was lucky enough to have people around me and resources given to me that helped me to finally break free. But I can say with full certainty it almost always leads to one of two destinations if it goes unchecked or the person goes unchanged.

The first is to a level of perversion that is almost impossible to come back from. I believe there are several issues in America today that are greatly hurting our society and can be linked directly and almost exclusively to pornography. Rape, large amounts of sexism, abortion, homosexuality, transgenderism, hook-up culture, large numbers of broken homes, pedophilia, and even more. You may not agree with me that some of these are problems with America today, but I can make pretty strong cases for all of these. And this is something I am planning on doing, but it will take many more words than what I can put in this chapter. So that will be another book for another time, hopefully not too far away.

The second is death. Plain and simple. I do think it can lead to spiritual death and other things of that sort, but I am talking about physical death. Another thing from my past that I am not afraid to talk about because I want it to help people is that I tried committing suicide on three seperate occasions. Once in high school, Once shortly after my oldest daughter was born, and the last time was probably about six or seven years back from the time of writing this. Two intentional attempted drug overdoses, and one interrupted attempt at getting a pistol.

For the first two it was very easy for me (after the fact) to see the direct connection to porn consumption. In highschool I hated myself because of it. I wanted to stop but realized I couldn't. It was consuming every aspect of my life so I tried to overdose on medication. It did not work.

The second time was shortly after my oldest daughter was born. I was a father now. I had a major responsibility. And I did not want to pass this along in any way to either this child or any future children. It was still consuming my life so I thought the best thing I could do for my daughter was to not be there. So this time I made sure it was going to work. I took a concoction of pills that should have easily killed someone even larger than me. I went to sleep not expecting to wake up. But I did. Did not even get sick. If I am being completely honest I have no idea how it happened except through the Grace of God.

The last time came after I had actually beaten my addiction. I was not looking at porn at all anymore, but I was still dealing with the side effects. Namely anxiety and depression. I was having some major marital problems (you'll read about that in a later chapter) had actually moved back into my parents house temporarily. But I just couldn't take it anymore. So one day I left work early, drove home, and had every intention of biting the barrel of one of my dad's handguns. But his gun cabinet was locked, and the key was not in the same place that he always kept it. As I was looking for another way to try and get into it, my parents randomly showed up. They left work early that day and had interrupted my plans. Obviously this led to some conversation that was very difficult for my parents to hear and also led me to get some much needed help.

I still deal with anxiety and depression, but they are not to the extent that I did before. But I also believe that the only reason I deal with them at all is because of my porn addiction.

I bring these instances up because they were all failures. Massive failures. But I have seen God use those failures in my life to help others. God has helped guide other men to freedom from that bondage through me by sharing my story. I have had the opportunity to provide guidance and wisdom through the leading of the Holy Spirit. And through my failure, and failure, and failure, and eventual success (not by my own might, but completely through God and his grace and mercy) others have seen there is hope for a better tomorrow.

Chapter 5

<u>Not Good Enough</u>

I don't think I have ever seen someone sad while eating fried chicken. And honestly that makes sense because fried chicken is probably my favorite food of all time. Especially if you throw in some mashed potatoes and buttermilk biscuits, that would easily be my favorite meal. And based on the success of the Kentucky Fried Chicken restaurant franchise I think it's easy to say I am not the only one who feels that way.

Colonel Harland Sanders has one of the most unique stories of all of them that I pulled for this book. If nothing else he definitely stands out for his age at the time that he had his eventual big success. But before we get into all of that, I want to go back and look at life for the Colonel before he was... well... The Colonel.

Harland Sanders had a rough start of things. His father died when he was only five years old. He dropped out of school around the age of twelve, then when he was fifteen he lied about his age in order to enlist in the military. He was sent to Cuba in order to serve as a mule handler but was honorably discharged after only four months. Once he got back Sanders had trouble keeping any job for very long. Then in 1930 when the Colonel was 40 years old he opened up a service station in Corbin Kentucky.

In this original service station there was not any seating. This meant people had to eat the food they ordered in his adjacent living quarters. But the popularity began to grow and eventually he had to move his operation into a nearby motel that would seat many more patrons at once. He spent the next 9 years perfecting his craft. Both learning how to best use the pressure cooker but also the best combination of herbs and spices. He finally landed on a special blend of herbs and spices that we now know today as "original recipe".

In 1949 he was given the name Colonel Sanders by the then governor of Kentucky. This is around the time he also started to finalize his signature look. Growing and bleaching a goatee and mustache, and starting to wear the white suits he is known for today.

In 1955 disaster would strike. As Interstate 75 was built it took traffic off of route 25 which is where his restaurant was located. He ended up selling the restaurant at auction and made just enough to pay off his debts. Now, at the age of 65, there really didn't seem to be much left to do. Starting over didn't seem to be an option, but he did have faith in his fried chicken recipe.

So at the age of 65, when most other people are looking forward to leaving the rat race, having their lives start to wind down, and entering retirement, Colonel Sanders would set out on a journey in his car to try and sell his recipe. He went from restaurant to restaurant trying to make this happen. He would cook his fried chicken for restaurant owners on the spot trying to show them how great this recipe was. It took him two years (yes two whole years) before he finally got someone to buy into his product and agree to sell his chicken in their store. Now beyond just being two years of traveling around, he was told no a whopping 1009 times before he received his first yes. Let me spell that out for you, one thousand and nine. That equals him being told no 1.38 times every single day for two years straight.

I cannot even imagine how I would have handled that situation. I don't think I would have made it to that first yes. Even after his chicken was a success in his original restaurant with local customers it would have been extremely demoralizing to take the idea nationally and see no success for that long. That is a very long time dealing with the idea of not being good enough. And that is what I would like to focus on with our next biblical story.

Before I get into the story I need to set something up first. I do not know how many people reading this book have knowledge of The Bible or not. So I need to explain something very quickly. The Bible was written by many different men, over the course of thousands of years, but it was directed by God. The Bible is broken up into several books split between the Old Testament and the New Testament. And a vast majority of the books in the New Testament were written by a man named Paul. The first time Paul is mentioned he is actually called Saul. It was not uncommon for someone to have dual names in those days. In Acts chapter 7 verse 58. To sum up what is going on, there is a Christian named Stephen who is in the process of being stoned to death by religious leaders because of his belief that Jesus was the Messiah and Saul is basically in charge of watching over their coats. So how did we go from Saul kind of participating in the death of a Christian to being a full on Christian hunter to finally having a name and life change and being responsible for writing most of the New Testament? Well I will tell you.

Acts 7 ends with Stephen taking his last breath and dying. Acts 8 opens with the line "And Saul approved of their killing him" The beginning of Chapter 8 talks about how persecution broke out against the early church, and Saul was very involved with this. Going from house to house and pulling both men and women out of their homes and sending them off to prison. Chapter 8 then shifts focus to another man and we pick back up with Saul in Chapter 9.

In case you were curious about if Saul's attitude towards christians had changed here is the opening line from Chapter 9 "Meanwhile, Saul was still breathing out murderous threats against the Lord's disciples" so that would be a no. Saul asks the High Priest for a letter to the synagogues at Damascus so that if he found any christians he would be able to take them back to Jerusalem as prisoners. He was a real go-getter! Then he sets off for Damascus in search of any of these "Christians" that are polluting the purity of his faith.

While on the way there he has a "road to Damascus experience". Actually the first "road to Damascus experience". I will trust that you can guess where the name comes from. The Bible says that a light from heaven flashed around him. Saul fell to the ground and heard a voice saying "Saul, Saul, why do you persecute me?" Saul asks "who are you Lord?" and the voice replies that they are Jesus, the same Jesus that he has been persecuting followers of. He then tells Saul to get up, go into the city, and he will be told what to do next.

Now Saul was not traveling alone. And it says the people traveling with him also heard this voice, but did not see anyone. Then Saul stands up and opens his eyes to discover he is now blind. So the people traveling with Saul had to lead him to the city and Saul was blind for three days.

Meanwhile, in Damascus, Jesus tells a man named Ananias to go to a house and ask for Saul from Tarsus and pray for him to restore his sight. I gotta say I do not really blame Ananias here because he is a little skeptical about going to Saul. He has heard about what Saul has been doing to christians and is really not feeling like he wants to go to prison, or die, or both. So Ananias airs his reservations about this plan and I love the response he gets.

Acts 9:15 - But the lord said to Ananias, "Go! This man is my chosen instrument to proclaim my name to the Gentiles and their kings and to the people of Israel."

Even though Saul had been traveling around with the express purpose of trying to snuff out christianity, God still had a purpose for him. And it was a very impactful purpose indeed. So on his way to try and wipe the belief in Christ, he has an encounter with Christ. Then Paul begins to pursue the conversion of others with as much tenacity as he previously pursued the condemnation of others. And the world would never be the same.

Just a side not to clarify, going forward I am going to be referring to Saul as Paul. As I stated previously the custom of having dual names was fairly common in this time. In Acts 13:9 The Bible references Saul "Then Saul, who was also called Paul" and from there on he is called Paul. So Saul and Paul were the same person and going forward I will be referring to him as Paul.

The purpose God had on Paul's life is still impacting people today. There are 27 total books in the New Testament and Paul wrote 13 of them. How much of that did Paul write? Well since you asked, I was curious too. I wanted to see what the percentage actually broke down to. So I found a word count (for the original languages) of how many words are in each book of the New Testament and did the math to see how much of the New Testament Paul wrote. If the totals I saw were correct there are 138,020 words in the New Testament, and 32,408 in the books Paul wrote. That figures out to Paul writing 23.48% of the New Testament. That is a pretty massive chunk.

I would also like to take a moment to notice something. One man who pursued God with absolutely everything he had. Never backing down from a situation or shying away from preaching the Gospel. One man led by the Holy Spirit impacted the world this much. How much could we impact the world if we today as Christians had the same devotion as Paul. I am calling out myself here as much as anyone else, but I thought this was a very interesting point to think about. And beyond the writing here, go read Acts 9. Just Acts 9 and see how much Paul did for and impacted the early church. It is crazy, and very encouraging, to see how much of an impact one person can have when they are being led by the Holy Spirit.

Now we never see this written in The Bible, but I can imagine there must have been times where Paul struggled. Thinking back at what he had done previously. When he watched over the coats of the men who stoned Stephen to death and approved of their actions. Not to mention all the other christians he had killed or thrown into jail. I can not help but think that Paul must have felt like he was not good enough. Even if it was not all the time, only periodically. The thought must have crept into his mind from time to time. The thought that he was not good enough to do what God had called him to do. But he still went on to play one of the biggest roles of anyone in the early church.

For most of my life I have struggled with a sense of not being good enough. Most of those feelings stem from failed relationships. This is probably the biggest and most influential struggle in my life. It has roots to every failure I've ever experienced. And through the years it has grown more and more prevalent in my life.

 I got married for the first time at a very young age. I was 19, she was 18. Straight out of highschool. We had kids very early. The Marriage lasted a total of six years. And although I would not change anything (because I got three beautiful children out of it) I can honestly say it was a horrible decision. And if I am being completely honest, it was probably one of the worst decisions of my life.

 Now I know what it probably sounds like, but no. I am not trying to paint the mother of my three oldest kids in a bad light. Looking back I do not believe either of us was ready for that level of relationship. We both fell short of where we needed to be and what we needed to do in order for the marriage to really work. And now we get along fairly well and are able to co-parent for our kids pretty effectively. We have both moved on and are happy in our relationships. And our kids have two loving households to call home.

 After this marriage ended I started talking to a few different girls, but did not have much luck. I was always much more serious about the relationship than they were, and I was willing to do whatever I could in order to show how serious I was. I spent a couple of thousand dollars in total on one. Bought a new phone for her when hers broke. Paying for meals, gifts, and other random stuff started to add up quickly. Me being used by people started to be a pretty common trend. But not much besides that ever really materialized until I started talking to who would become my second wife. I used a random name generator online to pick a random name for her, so going forward I will call her Tarah.

I can honestly say with no doubts whatsoever, that I jumped into this relationship very haphazardly. I was depressed and I hated being alone. Because of this I rationalized A LOT of red flags that popped up.

She had four kids of her own, and had been in an on again off again relationship with the father of three of those kids for several years. Tarah and I would start talking, then her ex would decide he wanted them to be together, so I would back off and they would try to work things out. Then he would go back to his other girlfriend he had at the time and Tarah and I would start talking again. This cycle went on for quite a while until we finally ended up moving past it. She moved in with me and we ended up getting married a month after that because I felt guilty about us living together and not being married.

Roughly two months after we got married we had the first major issue. Her ex (we will call him Joel going forward) had decided shortly after Tarah and I got married that he could not live without her. So he started texting her pretty much non stop. She decided she wanted her family back together so she was gonna go back to him. Two months in and this marriage was completely wrecked. Tarah was back to living with Joel.

Then about a week later it changed back. She had made a horrible mistake and just wanted to come back. So I let her. Because contrary to the statement I made in a previous chapter I was incredibly stupid. It was not long after we were back to living together before Tarah started cheating on me. And was doing so pretty regularly with Joel. Both at my house while I was gone, and at his house while his girlfriend was gone. They actually even took a couple trips together secretly so they could have time together as a couple. I know, I know. It is just soooo romantic!!

Now I want to take a quick pause here before I continue to explain something. You may not believe me, or see how it is possible, but I am not mad about this. I am not mad at Tarah or Joel. I have moved on completely from this situation. It hurt deeply at the time, but had this not happened I would not be where I am at currently in life, and I honestly could not be happier. I believe completely that God makes everything work together for good for those who are called according to his purpose. And this situation is included in that EVERYTHING. Because of this I am able to poke fun at my own mistakes and shortcomings. My goal of telling this story is not to shame others, or gain pity. It really is to show how I learned through failure, and eventually overcame it. Now where was I? Oh yes, the romantic endeavors of my then wife Tarah and her boyfriend Joel.

Probably the worst part of all of this happening is that shortly after Tarah and I had gotten back together I found out that she had cheated on me since we got back together. Then I found out that she was still continuing to cheat on me. But what did I do? Nothing. I pretended like I knew nothing. I had evidence. She had left her social media logged in on our computer. I sat down (actually to work on writing something) and saw messages back and forth that made it clear what was going on. But I did not confront them. I closed it out and pretended like I did not know. Because I did not want to accept that it was real, but I also did not want to face the difficult situation. So I pretended for about 7 months. Then we went back to the start. Tarah decided she just wanted to be alone and needed to work on herself and not be with anybody. I have come to realize that this meant the twenty-five minute drive between our house and Joel's house made it too difficult to sneak around so she was moving closer. We packed everything of hers and she was moved out in a matter of a couple weeks. We did not talk for a while after that happened, but that is not the end of the story.

After almost a year of no contact I got a random text from Tarah. I do not remember what it said, but it got us talking again. And honestly, things really seemed to be going differently. She seemed to actually be working to show me she was different. After about a month of talking again, I ended up moving into her apartment. We had never officially been divorced. I filed the paperwork, but never did anything else with it. So it just stopped and we remained married. But this time things really did seem to be different on her part.

After a couple months of being back together I started to notice some old behaviors creeping back up though. I did not have any definitive proof of an affair this time, but I noticed Tarah starting to be much more secretive with things. This went on for several months without me finding any evidence. I did bring my concerns up to her this time, but it was always dismissed with "If you forgive me you need to trust me again".

Again about a year into us being back together several things happened all one right after the other. Tarah got a new job and there were a couple of guys she worked with that I really felt uneasy about. An old friend of mine reached out to me and we started talking again. He actually lived pretty far away from me so we didn't see each other much, but we planned for him to come over one night and hang out. And we started to get along with Joel. But no matter what was going on I could not shake this overwhelming feeling I had that something was seriously wrong. I remember praying that if Tarah was cheating on me again it would be revealed to me definitively, and that I would have the courage to confront the situation and the wisdom to know how to handle it.

Then one day, completely out of the blue, Tarah just told me she was not happy and did not want to be together anymore. I was pretty shocked to say the least. I tried to talk through it. I wanted to try and find a way to save the marriage, but she was very set on what she wanted and it was very clear there was going to be no discussion about it. So I packed all of my stuff and was virtually moved out within a weekend. I had to move back in with my parents (which if you have never had to do again as an adult, let me just say it is a wonderful experience! Aaaaaaand sarcasm!)

To say I felt defeated and devastated was an understatement. I did not know what to do. I felt like there was something more I was not sure of but I could not pinpoint exactly what it was. Then people started coming out of the woodwork to pass along information to me. Now for the sake of time in this chapter and book I will not go into all of it, but I can summarize some.

I mentioned briefly the two guys she started working with that I felt uncomfortable about. I heard some rumors that she had been cheating on me with both of them. Now rumors are just that, and need to be taken with a grain of salt. But enough of the sources that passed information along to me are reliable that I feel confident saying she had been cheating on me with at least one of them. I found out that she had started cheating on me with Joel again as well. I do not think it was quite to the degree that it had been before, but it was definitely happening. And lastly, you remember the friend of mine that came over randomly one night? I can not confirm that there was a physical affair, but there was definitely an emotional affair going on. And it was definitely coming from both sides. So I got my answers, and I got my clarity on the situation. And needless to say I was destroyed.

Now through this difficult time I made the greatest decision of my life, definitely of my life up to that point. I was raised in church, have always attended but I was not really living like I was supposed to be. I was going through the motions and not giving my everything to the one who gave me everything. But once all of this had come crashing down on me I finally decided I was done trying to do this all on my own. I decided I was going to live completely sold out for God. See I did not want to live alone forever. I wanted to be married. I wanted to be with someone who actually wanted to be with me. I wanted to be with someone who valued me and loved me for me. Who was not just trying to use me and was not going to hurt me like I had been hurt before. But I had done pretty much as bad a job as anyone could have done in my search for that. So I was not going to do it anymore. I was done. I decided I was going to focus on God. I was going to live a life completely sold out to him, holding nothing back, and I would let him bring someone into my life that would be better than anything I could've ever imagined or wished for. So that is exactly what I did, and that is exactly what He did.

So the big final point I want to make here is this. Failure is not final. Failure does not have to define you. As we have gone through these stories, I hope I have done a good job showing these truths to you. I hope if you have disregarded yourself you will reconsider. I hope if you have disregarded The Bible you will reconsider that as well. Simply put I am not strong enough to do this on my own. I need help. Just like everyone else. And there is no one greater at turning failure into success than Jesus!

Chapter 6

Honesty! Integrity! And Sarcasm?

As I stated in a previous chapter I grew up in rural central Illinois. I know this may surprise some people but yes, there is a rural Illinois. I find when I tell people I am from Illinois they instantly think of Chicago. But Illinois is so much more than just the city of Chicago. We also have corn and corrupt politicians (especially governors) and corn! There is probably one thing that Illinois is more recognized for than Chicago though. You see it on every sign when you enter the state, and across the bottom of every license plate. Land of Lincoln. Side note, I was actually a little curious what it would generate so I googled "what is Illinois known for". I selected the first result and the top three on that list did not disappoint. Number one was Chicago, number two was Abraham Lincoln, and number three was corruption.

Yes, the man who was president during the civil war is from my home state. I have actually been to his childhood home, and there are several places close to where I grew up that had a lot of significance to Lincoln's earlier career. And of course with me being a bit of a history nut (especially American History) I love being so close to the "ground zero" of Lincoln's life. I would also like to point out as a little side note that my great grandfather's name (My Dad's Mom's Dad) was actually Jefferson Davis. And my wife actually grew up close to Irwin County GA, which is where Jefferson Davis was finally captured by Northern troops in the civil war. They have a museum setup in the place where he was captured that is very interesting to visit. My father in law actually proposed that my wife and I get married at the Museum. Since it was a Northern Yankee and and Southern Rebel coming together as one, that would be a fitting location

Probably best known for being the President that freed the slaves, Abraham Lincoln's life started far before he became the second greatest president our country has ever had (George Washington is first in case you were wondering, and those really are not debatable)

In 1838 he was defeated for the position of speaker of the house for Illinois House of Representatives. In 1843 he was defeated in his nomination to Congress. In 1848 he lost a renomination. In 1849 he was rejected for land officer. In 1854 he was defeated for the U.S. Senate. In 1856 he was defeated for nomination for Vice President. In 1858 he was once again defeated for the U.S. Senate. Then finally in 1860 he won election for President of the United States.

This is a very quick overview of Lincoln's political career focusing mainly on his losses. And most people that know anything about Abraham Lincoln will be fairly familiar with this. But I would like to focus on some other areas of his life. Some not as well known areas. Some of these may surprise you if you only know of the "Honest Abe" moniker. I can assure you the real Abe Lincoln was much more deep, mysterious, and controversial than most people realize. And that is what I would like the focus here to be on.

Eventually Abraham Lincoln became known for who he really was (for the most part). There are some minor details that may contradict the "Honest Abe" picture we have. But overwhelmingly Abraham Lincoln is known for being the President, or a politician in more general terms. And he is also known as being the president that ended slavery. Going forward I want to break this out into four small sections to focus on, and have a short story or stories for each. First is Lincoln as "Honest Abe". Second is Lincoln as quick witted. Third is Lincoln as a politician. And lastly Lincoln as anti-slavery.

First, Honest Abe. Lincoln had joined the Republican Party shortly after it was founded. Mainly because of their Anti-slavery stance. At the Republican National Convention in 1860 in Chicago the Republican presidential nominee would be chosen. The favorite to win, without a doubt, was William Seward. Lincoln did not attend. He had several individuals working for him that did though. They handed out large amounts of fake tickets to Lincoln supporters. Focused completely on packing the place with supports. Had multiple people yelling, screaming, and cheering for Lincoln above anyone and everyone else. The idea was to get as much support for old Abe on the floor as possible, then pull off whatever backroom deals necessary to get the nomination. Lincoln was aware of this but intentionally stayed home for "plausible deniability". I for one can say that while I do not support the tactics, I am very happy with the results. You could describe Lincoln getting the Republican nomination as many things, but accidental is not one of them. This really does kind of fly in the face of the "Honest Abe" name we have come to know. This is just one specific instance, but there are several others where we see examples of his somewhat sly nature.

Second, Lincoln as quick witted. This was not something I was really much aware of growing up. I did not actually learn about this attribute of Lincoln until at least highschool, but the man had an incredibly quick wit. Lincoln was publicly criticizing the Illinois State auditor James Shields in a newspaper under a pseudonym. Shields found out it was Lincoln and told him to apologize and publicly take back the comments or there would be a duel. Lincoln agreed to the duel and since he was being challenged he got to set the rules. It would not be a pistol duel, but a sword duel. Once shields arrived and they were all waiting to begin, Lincoln placed a board down and said neither of them could cross that line to attack the other. Then Lincoln begins stretching up with his sword and cutting off some particularly high branches of a nearby tree. Demonstrating his excessive wing span. This is enough to make shields reconsider and the two men agree to a truce. I think this story perfectly illustrates the brilliance and quick wit that Lincoln did have. I know I probably never would have considered this myself.

Third, Lincoln as a politician. Yes he was definitely most well known for his success as a president. But Honest Abe also spent 25 years as a Lawyer after he was admitted into the Illinois Bar. All of his training was informal, he would borrow books and study on his own. He actually was making a pretty good living for himself and his family as a lawyer before becoming president. From everything I have seen, read, and heard I have drawn the following conclusion. Abraham Lincoln was a politician, who sometimes made ends meet by being a lawyer. This is obviously entirely my opinion and I may be completely wrong, but it does seem to line up. No matter how well his law office was doing he felt the need to do more, like he was destined for something greater. And he kept coming back to politics again and again. I think this is who the real Lincoln was, and I wish we could have seen more of it. Or at least seen what a post civil war Lincoln presidency would have looked like. I do not think Lincoln was "pretending" to be something he wasn't when practicing law. But I do not believe that is what his real calling was, and that was simply a means to an end. I also believed that Lincoln knew this and that is why he tried multiple times with a "whatever it takes" attitude to get into the politics mainstream.

Lastly, Lincoln as anti-slavery. Lincoln states several times that he was against slavery as far back as he can remember, but the ultimate outcome of the civil war was not what he had intended when running for office. Actually in his debates with Stephen Douglas through Illinois Lincoln actually admitted that He thought slavery was morally wrong, but he also did not see blacks and whites as being equal. This opinion was obviously wrong, but it was based on lies pushed by the south in order to justify slavery.

Side note, this is a great example of what I discussed in the introduction. Abraham Lincoln was a great man, and he accomplished some great things. But not every belief he had or thing he did was great, or even good.

But the point I am making is that even when a lot of culture went the other direction, and it would have been probably much easier to go with them, Lincoln stood firm. He knew slavery was immoral and he did not back down from that. He was already aware of who he was, and he stuck with that instead of pretending to be something that he was not.

Next I want to revisit a previously mentioned person, but look at a slightly different situation in their life. If you remember in Chapter two I talked about the story of Jacob and Laban. How he worked for seven years for a wife he did not want, then another seven for one he did want. And the just fantastic love poetry he was speaking. I want to look at a little before that, and a little after that.

So Jacob was the second born. He actually had a twin brother named Esau. But God had already spoken and said he was going to enact his plan through Jacob, even though Esau was the first born. But this did not really sit well with Isaac (their father). Esau was his favorite, so his plan was to bless Esau instead of Jacob. We pick up their story in Genesis 27. Isaac was old and his eyesight was pretty well shot. He tells Esau to go hunt some wild game for him, and prepare a meal for him so he can eat then bless Esau before he dies.

Esau leaves to go do this but the instructions were overheard by Rebekah (their mother). She had a favorite as well, but her favorite was Jacob. So she cooks a meal just like Isaac likes then helps her son Jacob deceive Isaac. They put goatskins on his arms to make him feel like Esau, because Esau was a hairy dude. He also wears Esau's clothes so he smells like Esau as well. Jacob goes in to his father, who is instantly suspicious because it does not sound like Esau. But Isaac feels his arms and the goatskins deceive him. Because once again, Esau was a hairy dude. Then Jacob goes in closer and Isaac smells Esau's clothes and is fully convinced that this is his son Esau. So he blesses him on the spot. I do want to quote this whole blessing, because I think it is good to see what all was really at stake here. We'll start in verse 27.

²⁷ So he went to him and kissed him. When Isaac caught the smell of his clothes, he blessed him and said,
"Ah the smell of my son is like the smell of a field that the Lord has blessed.

²⁸ May God give you heaven's dew and earth's richness - an abundance of grain and new wine.

²⁹ May nations serve you and people bow down to you. Be lord over your brothers, and may the sons of your mother bow down to you. May those who curse you be cursed and those who bless you be blessed."

The next thing we read says that Jacob left Isaac and almost as soon as he does Esau comes in. Esau and Jacob put two and two together and realize it was Jacob who stole the birthright. Esau is pretty heated over this, and understandably so. He quite literally just had everything taken from him. He vows to kill Jacob once his father dies and the time for mourning his father is over. Rebekah was told about this reaction and goes to Jacob and sends him off and that is where we saw Jacob meet up with Laban.

This first story of Jacob shows us the beginning of what really defined Jacob's life. Trying to be someone or something that he is not. Using deceit in the process as well. I am sure that Jacob had to be aware that God had already said the promise was going to be fulfilled through him, not Esau. But rather than let God work his plan out on his own, Jacob decided to take matters into his own hands. He did have some encouragement from mommy dearest. I mean she did come up with the plan in the first place and kind of set the whole thing into motion. But regardless of that, Jacob is responsible for his actions. He decided to take the steps to deceive his father into getting what God had already stated was his.

The main thing I want to focus on in this chapter is not trying to be something that you are not, but I think there is another important lesson here as well. Several years ago I attended a church that was led by a man named Pastor Randy. I am not sure if he knows this or not but he was probably one of the most influential people in my faith and christian walk. But I brought him up because of a saying he had that I still hold to today. "Don't doubt in the dark what God revealed in the light." Very simple, but I believe this is also very profound. And I think what we see in the story here is a prime example of not listening to that advice. Jacob knew the promise God had made. The faith should have been there to trust that God would bring everything around to his plan on his own. But one thing I have seen proven in my life is that God rarely works without man's negative involvement.

Even though Jacob's ultimate goal lined up with God's plan, the actions to get there were not acceptable. And because he decided to take matters into his own hands it caused major problems for his family. He would leave his home and would not return for two decades. Honestly never really have a good relationship with his brother. And he never saw his mother again after this.

We see later on that Jacob makes a promise basically saying that he will follow God if God protects him. First of all I would advise against this type of dealing with God. I think it goes without saying, but I will say it anyway. We are not in a position to negotiate with the Almighty. We can ask Him for things such as safety, health, protection, provision. That is part of prayer and I think God wants us to come to him with our needs, wants, and desires. But that is a far cry from coming at it like a negotiation. Secondly we can see in a couple instances that Jacob refers to God as "The God of my father". There is some obvious distance there but (spoiler alert) that gap is going to be closed later on.

The next story of Jacob I want to look at takes place after the story with Laban. In Genesis 32. He is finally free, and is actually on his way back home. I think as Jacob leaves it is an awesome display of how powerful and how in control God actually is. When Jacob first came here he had nothing but a staff. He met God on his way, and God stayed with him and provided for him. Blessed whatever he did and now as he is leaving Jacob has a multitude going with him. He sent ahead some servants to meet his brother Esau and basically give him a heads up that Jacob was coming back, but this was done with humility. They tell Esau that "His servant Jacob is on his way". Jacob's servants return to tell Jacob that Esau is coming to meet him and there are 400 men with him.

Keep in mind the last contact Jacob had with Esau was getting the heck outta dodge because he Esau was going to murder him. So Jacob splits the group he is traveling with into two groups, so if one is attacked the other may be able to get away. He also sends groups of animals and other things as gifts for Esau, in hopes of buying some good favor from him. Then starting in verse 9 Jacob prayed this prayer.

⁹ Jacob said, "O God of my father Abraham and God of my father Isaac, O LORD, who said to me, 'Return to your country and to your relatives, and I will prosper you,' ¹⁰ I am unworthy of all the lovingkindness and of all the faithfulness which You have shown to Your servant; for with my staff only I crossed the Jordan, and now I have become two companies. ¹¹ Deliver me, I pray, from the hand of my brother, from the hand of Esau; for I fear him, that he will come and attack me and the mothers with the children. ¹² For You said, 'I will surely prosper you and make your descendants as the sand of the sea, which is too great to be numbered.' "

Now this is more like it. The humility on display here by Jacob is really something I think we can strive for. But he has also started to remember what God promised. Even if the situation looks bleak, he is holding onto the promise God made. And God always keeps his promises. I have actually done something similar to this from time to time. While praying, I bring up some of the promises God has made to us in his word. I am not doing this to remind God of any promise, he does not need me to remind him. Honestly it is more for myself than anything. So as I am praying through a difficult situation like we see Jacob in here, or Joseph previously, or any other difficult situation I may bring to God I do not understand what is going on in my situation, but I do know he promises in Romans 8:28 that he makes all things work together for good to those that love Him and are called according to His purpose. So even though I may not see any positives in the current situation, I know he can bring it out.

But let's get back to Jacob. He gets to a point where he sends everyone that is with him and everything that he owns across this river, then he is alone. Picking up in verse 24.

²⁴ Then Jacob was left alone, and a man wrestled with him until daybreak. ²⁵ When he saw that he had not prevailed against him, he touched the socket of his thigh; so the socket of Jacob's thigh was dislocated while he wrestled with him. ²⁶ Then he said, "Let me go, for the dawn is breaking." But he said, "I will not let you go unless you bless me." ²⁷ So he said to him, "What is your

name?" And he said, "Jacob." **28** He said, "Your name shall no longer be Jacob, but Israel; for you have striven with God and with men and have prevailed."

I see verse 27 here as a direct callback to Genesis 27:18 when he goes into his fathers tent and Isaac asks who he is. It can be so easy to forget these were real people that had real feelings and emotions. I can just imagine, as Jacob is making this journey. Thinking continuously about the last time he was at home. How he deceived his family and cheated his brother. Then when he finally is able to be honest about who he is it changes. Jacob means supplanter. One who seizes, circumvents, or usurps. Israel means God contends. And his lineage Would become God's chosen people.

God can't bless who you pretend to be. So once Jacob came to terms with his faults, or who he really was, then God blessed him. I believe our society has a major identity crisis (and I do not just mean people who think they are the opposite gender. Although that is a problem, I will leave it for the next book). People spend money they don't have, to buy stuff they don't want, to impress people they don't like. Comparison is not something that is generally healthy or good. At least not in the most part with how it is handled in the First world.

I don't have a really in depth personal story for this one. More of a general mindset I have struggled with and then when it finally broke off of me. In the previous chapter I talked about how I struggled for a long time with feeling like I was not good enough. A lot of that started in the chapter before that with addiction and is also rooted in comparison. I am a very competitive individual by nature. I am always competing against anyone and anything that I can. Even if they are not aware. This can, on some occasions and has in me, led to a very strong personal drive and hard work ethic. But there are two heads to this monster.

Comparison can be deadly. Especially in areas where you should be content. There may be men reading this that are steeped in an addiction to pornography like I use to be. But worse yet, you are married to a woman who is kind, compassionate, loving, caring, and treats you well. She is a biblical representation of what a wife should be. And porn has you comparing the best thing that ever happened to you, to something that never actually happened to you.

Or take a person who is following their dream. Like him or not you really can't argue that Michael Jackson was not one of the best performers of his generation. But what if he spent his entire life trying to emulate the Beatles? Or Frank Sinatra. Constantly comparing what he was doing to why they did. He probably would have quit and if not he almost definitely wouldn't have reached the level that he did. Then we would never know about Billie Jean!

I believe it was Albert Einstein who said "everyone is a genius, but if you judge a fish by his ability to climb a tree it will spend its whole life believing it is stupid". You do not have to be everyone else, or anyone else. God created you to be you. There is a purpose, a plan, and a future all tied to the person you really are.

As I said previously I struggled with this for a long time. Actually up to the point of starting this book I was still struggling with this. In order to explain what happened to make it stop I need to give a little back story.

About a year and a half years ago I left the church I was at because Tiffany and I were getting married and would be attending the church she was on staff at. I had led worship at this church for about 10 years prior to leaving. But it was always in a volunteer capacity. After I started attending the new church I very quickly became acquainted with Andreas. He is the worship pastor. Since I had been one previously and knew how to play some instruments I quickly found myself jumping in on the worship team. Andreas is also completely unaware that I am putting this little story in this book, but he is one that is editing for me. So if you are reading this when the book is published that means Andreas approved!

I mentioned previously that I can play several instruments, but I am entirely self taught, play mostly by ear, and I cannot read music. On top of that my level of expertise when it comes to music theory, composition, how chords are built, anything even remotely like that is a big fat zero. Zilch. Nada. I do not get it. I have tried on several occasions to learn more about it, but for some reason it just never stuck.

Andreas on the other hand was very much different. Not only does he have a sweet German accent (he comes straight from the motherland). But he also has an in-depth knowledge of most of this, definitely far beyond anything I could hope to have. He also has been able to do much more to bring the worship team at my new church further than I could at my previous church.

HOW TO FAIL AT PRACTICALLY EVERYTHING: A COMPREHENSIVE GUIDE

In short, Andreas was better at this than I ever could have been in every single measurable way.

Now I never had any bitterness, contempt, or any negative feeling towards Andreas whatsoever. He is honestly probably my closest friend aside from my wife. And definitely one of the few people that I actually enjoy spending time around. And Andreas never did anything to make me feel any of this. But it started leading me to be very very down on myself. Simply because of the comparison I was making.

Then it finally stopped one day. I remember I was praying about direction. I was needing guidance on my job, we were looking to move to a new house, and several other things. But I really started praying about my calling. I did not know what it was. Did not know what I was supposed to do. But I did have this nagging feeling like I was missing out on something. I could not put my finger on it. But I remember after praying for all of these things, getting up, getting in my car, and heading to work for that day. I was thinking about what I had prayed about, specifically my calling. Then my train of thoughts led me to "I could never be the worship leader Andreas is". Then I heard God say "That's good because I did not call you to be Andreas, I called you to be Jesse".

If you have never had an experience like this it is kind of hard to explain. I did not hear an audible voice. The best comparison I can give is like I had a thought, but it was clear it was not my own thought. I know how entirely crazy this sounds if you are not familiar with it, but it is my story, and it is true.

After I heard this I was just quiet. Did not do much the rest of my way to work. Just really thought about what I heard and how much time I had spent focusing on that. Not just in this one situation, but comparison going back years, decades even. I began to wonder how many opportunities I had squandered because I did not think I could compare with someone else. When I was never supposed to even be in the same lane as them.

That is part of what led me back to writing this book. I actually started this after failing at something I had put a good deal of effort into. And I was not writing this book to publish or to even be of help to people. I was mad at myself. It seemed the only thing I was good at was not being good at stuff. So I began writing this book. Initially as a sarcastic, self-deprecation project. Then I started seeing real positives that could come from it. Then when I had this moment, it kicked this book into high gear. I guess my takeaway here is this. Yes you can model yourself to be like others in some ways, but ultimately you need to realize you are not them. You are you, that is entirely different from anyone else. A God given purpose that no one else on earth is called to fulfill. So seek God, find what it is, and follow him into it. If you do that, you will never be disappointed.

Chapter 7

<u>What Happened In 1492?</u>

In one way or another you have been lied to for practically your entire life. A phrase that was common in my history class was "the winner writes the history books'". And this statement is true, but it does not stop with just talking about war. Many times what we read in history is very watered down and skewed in one way or another. A good practice to get into if you are looking into these things is to find primary (or as close to primary as you can get) documents. So first or second hand accounts of what happened. One very bad practice is to just take the word of people on social media or other such avenues to hear the truth about topics. Especially recently.

There have been a lot of historical figures that were very recently painted in a bad light. I alluded to this in the introduction of the book in reference to Lynn Manuel Miranda's portrayal of Thomas Jefferson. But I would like to look at another figure, someone a little earlier than President Jefferson. Back in 1492. A certain someone sailed the ocean blue.

That was a phrase I think most kids who attended public school were probably aware of. But recently we have seen Christopher Columbus painted in a much different light. People refusing to celebrate Columbus day. Statues being torn down. Even cities are considering renaming themselves because they hold the name of one of the bravest men to ever live.

I remember even seeing Greg Poppovich (Historically great basketball coach) recently, ranting after a game about it. Said he did not understand why the city of San Antonio school district celebrated "Indigenous people/ Columbus Day". Because Columbus "initiated a new world genocide". But he gives the San Antonio school credit a little because at least they added the "Indigenous people's day". Said he is amazed that their city is "that backwards" that they still include Columbus in it. Well I would first like to ask which Indigenous people are we celebrating? Is it the Taíno Indians who Columbus first met when he landed in the Bahamas? The ones that Columbus demanded his crew treat with kindness and respect? Or could they mean the Caribs? Which were the second main tribe that Columbus came in contact with. The Caribs were known for two things. Making elegant cotton rugs, and eating people. This behavior explained the scars on some of the Taíno's bodies. The Caribs also considered babies (both born and unborn) to be a particular delicacy.

The truth is that the negative rhetoric about Columbus comes almost exclusively from a single document that was discovered in 2015 that was published by his chief political rival. It would be like us uncovering a long lost tweet from Donald Trump talking about how horrible Hillary Clinton was and using that as the definitive proof that she was a horrible person. Whether you agree with that statement or not I hope you can see the flawed logic there.

Columbus did do some bad things, usually against his wishes. But he was also in a much different world than we were. So we should not judge him based on our standards. People also forget all the great things Columbus did. If not for his brave trek across the unknown Most of the people alive in the world today probably would not be. He really created the Latino people group. And he even adopted the son of a Native American and raised him as his own.

Yes I would say the backlash over everything Christopher Columbus is a little... well... stupid. I encourage anyone reading this book as well, do not just take my word for it. Go do the research yourself. Actually look up the historical documents, do some reading, and don't just listen to the dude on tik tok who sounds confident and acts like he knows what he is talking about. Because he probably does not. I don't think you should just take my word for it either. A simple google search can put most of these documents at your fingertips.

I think it is clear from the writings of Columbus that he believed he was on a mission from God. And there was a rather strange event that happened that makes it seem as though that was indeed the case.

While on the Voyage, Columbus had to stop several attempts by his crew to turn the ship around and go back home. But Columbus was able to keep the mission alive through all of these. Then on the evening of October 11, 1492 Columbus spotted something. In the distance he spotted a light. He described it as looking like a small candle that rose and lifted up. He grabbed two others to see if they could see it, one could and one could not. The natural thought was that this was some type of fire on land. But given the distance they still were from land, that doesn't seem possible. They did not end up landing in the Bahamas until the next day. There are some possible explanations that have been floated as to what this light could have been, but I personally do not find any of them very convincing. Is it possible that God was guiding a journey, through some severely lonely wilderness, with a type of fire? Well he has done it before!

I am not trying to say without a doubt that Columbus was being guided by God Almighty to find the Americas, but I do think it is a rather interesting idea to throw around. And I fully plan on asking one of these days when I get there. But what I really wanted to focus on here was Columbus' attitude throughout everything. He had some serious hardships in his life. Mistreatment & misrepresentation seemed to occur regularly. Especially when it came to Columbus trying to govern on dry ground. But through it all his attitude remained the same. If I could use only one word I believe steadfast or unapologetic both fit rather appropriately. And I think we see that in his famous *Lettera Rarissima* Where he quite famously told his critics (in a very eloquent way) to "go to hell".

I think it goes without saying that while I agree with the mindset of pushing invaluable negative comments to the side, I do not agree with how Columbus chose to do so in this letter. I do think it is very important to be able to do in life though. This is kind of the reverse of what I opened with in Chapter 1. And while it is important to find the people that you need to listen to. People that have your best interest at heart. People that love you enough to hurt your feelings sometimes. I believe it is equally important to shut out the people that are not on that list. Sometimes well meaning people are the worst to listen to. Like Peter telling Jesus he does not need to go to the cross, and Jesus replied "get behind me Satan". We should likewise be able to spot bad advice, comments, or criticism. Even if it sounds good. And move on without it.

I think it goes without saying that there were many things that Columbus saw on his journey that were brand new. Both to him, the others on his ship, and everyone back in the world they knew. But there is one thing that I am sure he saw that really stands out. Rain! Yep. I am sure Columbus saw a good amount of rain. Both on the trip and after he arrived in the new world. But why is rain so special? Well I will tell you the truth. Columbus seeing rain is a big deal because I needed it to segway into the next part of this chapter.

Rain can be viewed in different ways depending on where you are in the world, and your specific circumstances. But pretty much everyone in the world is familiar with it. There was however a time where that was not the case. Next

I want to look at the time that rain first fell on the earth. We are going to look at the story of Noah.

Let's look first in Genesis chapter 6. To summarize, man was really bad. Like really really bad. So bad that God wanted to wipe man out. But there was one man who found favor in God's eyes. That man was Noah. God told Noah that the whole earth was wicked and evil and he was going to destroy them all because of that. But before he did, he gave Noah some instructions. Specifically to build a boat. A giant boat. You could say that this is where Noah's real story ARK began. Yes I know that is comedic gold, and now that you've stopped laughing we will continue.

God did not just leave Noah high and dry though. He gave him specific instructions for how big the boat should be, what it should be made out of, and even what he was to take with him on the Ark. This would have been a major undertaking. There is some debate about exactly how long it took. But given the dimensions (45 foot high, 450 foot long, and 75 foot wide), the technology available at the time, and the workers present (at most it was Noah and his family) I think it is safe to say this was at least a several decade long project.

There are some things that we (people in the church that have heard this story before) kind of assume as being true, but we really do not have evidence for. One of those things is that people mocked Noah. There really is not any indication in the Bible of that being the case. But another that I have heard several times is that Noah preached to the people of his time about turning from their wicked ways and the coming judgment. Both of these are things that I personally believe, but I hold those beliefs loosely. There is 2 Peter 2:15 which says that Noah was a "preacher of righteousness" but this does not necessarily have to pertain to warning people about the flood. Noah was around 500 years old when God told him about the flood, so it is entirely possible this passage is referring to actions of his prior to building the ark.

Regardless, It is my opinion that people were probably mocking (or at the very least doubting his mental capacity) during the construction of the ark. The massive size of the boat would have made it difficult to not notice. And just knowing the nature of people in general, unkind words were probably exchanged. But that did not change what Noah did. The Arc was still built. Animals placed on it, along with Noah and his family. Up until this point rain had not fallen on the earth. We see a little earlier in Genesis that moisture would rise up from the earth to water plants and things like that.

Now there are some people who think this was only an occurrence inside the actual Garden Of Eden. And even if that is true it does not really change the story or the point I am making very much. Because regardless of how water got to the surface of the earth previously, we had never seen a flood like this before. I imagine there was much shock and horror as the water began to rise and people started to run for the boat they saw in the distance. Trying desperately to seek refuge with the man they mocked for so many years. I have heard it said before "Everyone thinks you're crazy, until it starts to rain".

Again, I want to reiterate, the Bible does not expressly say that people were mocking Noah, or even saying anything negative towards him at all. That is an assumption on my part. But I do believe it is likely, and I do think there is a good lesson to take from it. Noah heard from God, and that was all that mattered. Once he got his instructions, nothing was going to sway him. The confidence he had in God to complete a seemingly impossible task is something I strive to have myself. I have already stressed the importance of listening to people. But now I want to stress the importance of not listening to people. I know, I know. I am just being so incredibly straightforward with all of this instruction.

So I talked in Chapter 1 about how I used to care far too much about what other people thought of me. I also mentioned that now I have gone in the complete opposite direction. Almost to a fault. I am fully willing to admit that I should probably care a little more about how I am perceived by people. But I do also think there is a benefit to being able to speak directly, bluntly, clearly, and even abrasively if necessary. This is one area where my wife and I actually balance each other out quite well. She reminds me that sometimes I come across as a complete jerk, and I remind her that sometimes she goes too far to try and not hurt someone's feelings. Like I said before, people who truly love and care about you will not be afraid to hurt your feelings sometimes. And you will be much better for it too.

I do not remember exactly when the shift in how much I care about other people's opinions began or ended. I can clearly remember being extremely overly concerned with it, then I remember not really caring at all. I do believe this shift was a result of some negativity that I suffered through. Relationships have frequently been a source of pain in my life. And in some cases I would even say a source of trauma. For a long time I was very quick to trust, I wore my heart on my sleeve, and I was incredibly giving as well.

I have mentioned a couple of examples briefly in previous chapters. Between allowing myself to be a doormat to others, and jumping at the opportunity to shell out thousands of dollars to help people who were very clearly only using me, I finally just decided I was done. I did not want to go through it anymore, and one of the best ways to do that was to not care about what other people thought. If something hurt me or upset me I decided I was just going to be blunt about it. No beating around the bush or trying to tiptoe around it. No passive aggressive comments or conversations. I am just going to clearly state what I am thinking and leave it at that. And I think for the most part it has really served me well since I began doing so.

I have a couple examples I would like to bring up, one from my own life and one relating to something in my life, to demonstrate how not being concerned with others opinions has actually been incredibly beneficial at certain times..

This first is with what I believe as a Christian and conveying that to a world that does not believe the same. This may end up being somewhat controversial but honestly it really should not be. I recently saw a 60 minutes interview where Anderson Cooper was interviewing Bart Barber. Barber had recently been voted the president of the Southern Baptist Convention (SBC). And this is coming hot on the heels of some major sexual assault issues that were going on, unaddressed within the organization and some of the church's that fall within the SBC. Obviously this was something that Anderson Cooper was going to bring up and I loved president Barber's answer. He condemned it. No questions, no gray area, nothing. Explicitly condemned all of it. And that is exactly what needed to happen. I think there are too many people (especially in politics and the church) that want to dance around topics instead of being straight forward. I do not necessarily agree with everything he said in the interview, but overall I was good with it. But what really stuck out to me is what happened when THE questions was asked.

It is not a secret that the culture in America right now is very pro LGBT, and pro choice. Anytime any main news outlet interviews a Christian there are two questions involving these topics that almost always come up. And by almost always I do not mean like 75% of the time. We are talking like 99% of the time. So I really think Barber had to be aware he was going to be asked these questions. Especially knowing that Anderson Cooper has been very outspoken about the fact that he is a homosexual man.

The first of these two questions that was asked was something about a specific situation that took place in Ohio. I do not know all the specifics of the situation, but to my understanding there was a ten year old girl who was raped, and ended up getting pregnant as a result of the rape. But because Roe V. Wade got overturned, she was not able to get an abortion in her home state. Cooper asks Barber how he views this sexual abuse of a child and specifically making that ten year old girl carry this baby to term and deliver the baby as opposed to letting her get an abortion. Barber responds that he sees that as horrible, but I see it as preferable to killing someone else. And this answer was spot on. As horrible as that situation is, it does not justify murdering the unborn baby that is in the womb. If anyone in that situation deserves the death penalty it is the man who raped a ten year old little girl. My personal opinion is that rapists should either be castrated or killed. No door #3. And I think if we were a little more harsh on people who did heinous acts like this, especially towards children, we would have much fewer instances of it happening.

The next question is the one that really ALWAYS pops up. Maybe not the exact questions that Anderson Cooper asks, but some form of it always ends up being asked whenever christians are interviewed. I have been very frustrated in the past watching some christians just completely mishandle this question. Some of that could be because they were not necessarily prepared to answer the question, but given how often it comes up I do not think that is a valid excuse. I think the more likely answer is that they are too concerned with what culture, or the secular community will think of them if they give the answer they know the Bible really gives on the topic.

First Cooper asks if gay people should be converted out of being gay. To which Barber responds that sinners should be converted out of being sinners and that applies to everyone. A+ response. He answered Coopers question, addressing homosexuality as a sin, but also addressed that everyone is a sinner, and homosexuality is just one way that we as man kind have sinned against an almighty God.

Cooper then comes back and asks if someone can be a "good christian" and be a member of the SBC and married to a member of the same sex. Barber responded with a very clear and concise "no". He then went on to explain why that was his answer, but he did not beat around the bush. He did not tiptoe around the subject trying to appease Anderson Cooper without "technically" lying about what the Bible says. It is rather clear that both abortion and homosexuality are both condemned outright in the Bible. And Barber made no qualms about it.

As a Christian in a culture like we have in America today, this is not only necessary, but sadly incredibly rare. There are many that believe these, and many other things like these. Beliefs that run counter to the culture. That is what christianity has always done. But there are so few people who are willing to take a stance on what God's word says. No matter what others may think, or how they will be perceived.

What we need to get better about realizing is this. The truth is still true, regardless of how it makes you feel. The truth is also still true, regardless of if you believe it or not. Makes me think of a lyric from a Rapper called NF. If you have not heard of him, I highly suggest you check him out. But in a song called "Real" he has a lyric "If God ain't real, then real isn't". God is absolute truth. And the Bible is his word. So as a Christian, how selfish is it to blow off an opportunity to acknowledge sin for what it is. Then take that as an opportunity to go on to talk about how ALL sin, not just homosexuality, leads to eternal damnation and suffering in hell. But God provided a way of escape. He loved us so much that he sent his son to take that punishment in our place, so that we may live eternally with him.

I have seen Christian after Christian after Christian completely fumble this question when it is presented. Either flat out deny the truth in the Bible or tiptoe around it as I said earlier. Things like "well I just believe God loves everyone". While that is true it fails to address the fact that salvation is not achieved without accepting Jesus' work on the cross, confessing your sin, and turning from it to walk towards God. Or one that really gets under my skin "well it's not my place to judge". Also technically true, but telling someone the truth about the eternal ramifications of their choices is not judging them. It is actually trying to help prevent a far worse fate through judgment that is coming later. I think it is clear that I am passionate about people standing in truth and doing so on the authority given to them through Jesus.

The second is more concerned with how I interact with other christians. This is something I think the church has gotten mixed up pretty badly in the last several decades, or maybe even further back. If we look at the example of Jesus I believe we would be doing many things differently. Jesus was much more abrasive with people in the "church" than he was with those outside of it. Now, I am not saying that he did not address sin in other people's lives, because he definitely did. But he did seem to be more direct, blunt, and abrasive with the religious leaders of the day. Why was that? They knew better. They had God's law, had studied it their whole lives, and were trying to find loopholes to get as close to sin as possible. Oftentimes stepping over the line, or making up new and unnecessary guidelines for people too.

We actually have an amazing outline in the bible about how we are to act out discipline inside the church. Both as a leader offering correction to a congregation member. But even how to handle a situation in which a leader is in the wrong. There are outlines for the minimum requirements of those in leadership as well. And many Christians have absolutely no idea about any of this. As an example, in Matthew 18 Jesus gives some advice on dealing with people in the church who have sinned. First go to them in private. If they do not listen, then take a couple of people with you and address it again. If they still do not listen then the church as a whole is to address the person. And if after that they still do not listen then they are to be treated as an unbeliever.

In 1 Corinthians 5 we see another example from Paul here. There is a situation where a member of the church is in some pretty serious sexual immorality. And Paul addresses it sharply. A man is sleeping with his father's wife. This could be an incestuous relationship or it could be a step mother. But either way, it is wrong. Paul tells them that they should be in mourning over this and this man should have been kicked out of the church.

I have kind of started feeling a call recently to handle some things like this of my own. Maybe not specifically these situations, but teaching proper ways to handle things in the church. Addressing issues that arise. And doing so in a way that helps to bring health to the church. But even more than just that, actually showing others how to do the same and to stand in the authority God has given us.

As I have been feeling this leading, and also praying about it I have actually had a situation pop up in my life that calls for this exact thing. I will refrain from naming any names or going into too many specifics while telling this story. I have a friend who is in a position of ministry. Let's call him Fred. Fred recently brought up a book that he thinks I should read because he thinks it would challenge me, but in a good way. For the sake of anonymity I am also not going to mention the name of the book. May seem like a little overkill, but naming the book specifically would give away the person too.

I can say though, that this book is regarding Bethel church in California. The substance of the book is talking about things that are done at the church and how they are done. I have seen that there are some positives in this book, but there are also many many negatives. My biggest concern though is in me knowing other stuff about Bethel that I do. Now if you are not a Christian and are not familiar with some "Christianese" then I may lose you in some of what is coming up, but please try to stay with me if at all possible.

I do not like to make assumptions about other people's salvation status but I feel for the sake of argument here it is needed. I believe Bill Johnson (the Apostle for Bethel Church) is a born again believer. I believe him and most others at his church are honestly seeking God, and trying to enact his will on earth. I believe they want to see souls saved for the kingdom of heaven. But I also believe Bethel is promoting and approving of some things that are incredibly dangerous.

I have seen some teaching of Bethel as well as some of their own books that they have published that are talking about some very concerning things. Bethel is trying to go into the New Age and take things back for God, but these are things that were never in line with anything God had for his people. Actually some of what I have seen them promoting and approving of is borderline demonic at best. I believe Bethel has put such a hyper focus on Revival and specifically a couple of gifts of the spirit, that they are sacrificing discernment in the process.

But back to Fred. I have noticed some things in Fred, prior to him bringing up the book, that had kind of concerned me. But after the book recommendation it took that concern even further. I will be honest, I actually did not want to address this. I did not think that I was in a position to actually speak about this concern in a way that would make Fred at the very least re-evaluate some of the things he has been pursuing. So I was not going to say anything. But I started feeling convicted about it. Then when we had a short conversation in passing about it, that conviction grew even more.

So I have not actually had the conversation yet, but I am going to. I am going to get the book that was recommended and I am going to read through it entirely. In the process of doing so I am going to make notes, and pull specific scripture that refutes some of the claims that are made. Again because I have no authority in and of myself. The only authority I have was given to me through God and his word. If I do not stand on that, I have no solid ground.

The point I want to make to bring this chapter to a close is that this conversation is probably not going to be easy. Nothing against Fred, but no one really likes to be told they are wrong. Especially not when they have been studying something and believe they are actually onto a secret positive thing that can have a major positive impact. But I am hopeful that the Holy Spirit is going to guide my words, and open his heart. At the end of the day I have to do what I feel God is leading me to do. And that takes precedence over anyone's feelings, including my own.

Chapter 8

It's Pronounced Leviosa, Not Leviosa!

If you are one of the many many people who have watched and enjoyed the Harry Potter franchise you probably read those two words, spelled exactly the same, and pronounced them differently in your head. You also probably read it in the voice of a nearly twelve year old Hermione Granger.

J.K. Rowling is without a doubt one of the most influential writers of the last several decades and quite possibly even further back than that. There really is not much room for debate on that statement, but there are a couple of possibly controversial issues I want to address at the onset of this chapter. If you fall into one of these categories then please hear me out on this.

This first thing I would like to address will be almost exclusively from people who are christian that claim Harry Potter is evil witchcraft and sorcery. This is a topic that is highly debated in a lot of christian circles. I have many friends that fall on both sides of this argument, and I love them all dearly. My stance on the subject is this. While the bible does say that witchcraft is evil, I think claiming that watching Harry Potter as being included in that is a little bit of a stretch. I would actually love to sit down and break down all the specifics of why I hold this stance, but I will summarize it for the sake of time in this book. My main argument is that the "magic" and "witchcraft" we see in Harry Potter is not the same as what is being condemned in the Bible. It is actually completely made up and completely fiction. The spells are actually just Latin words for things. As an example Lumos is a spell that creates light from the end of a wizard's wand. Lumos is taken from the Latin Lumen, which literally translates to light or lamp. Pretty simple stuff.

I think the fact that this is complete fiction, and not really based on realistic witchcraft makes it a gray area at best. But I also believe if you take this stance on Harry Potter, you would have to take the same stance on Lord of The Rings, Chronicles of Narnia, Star Wars, and Marvel. All of which have Witches of some kind and the use of magic, spells, and or sorcery. Maybe you agree with that and are willing to make the stance I have outlined here. If so, that is fine. The Bible does say that sometimes the Holy Spirit convicts us of things that maybe are not considered sin for everyone, and we should listen to those convictions. But I do not believe you can make a very strong Biblical case that it is wrong for everyone, and if we go back to the last chapter, that is what we need to do when confronting issues like this. If you can't do that then you are just stating your opinion.

Beyond this I think that Harry Potter actually teaches some very good Christian principles. Below are some examples of Christian teachings we can actually see played out in the story of Harry Potter.

1. Teaching that self sacrifice & putting others needs above yourself is a heroic action.
2. True love is extremely powerful.
3. Real good will always conquer evil in the end.

The next controversial issue I want to address is that J.K. Rowling recently came under fire for some stances she made publicly about the transgender community. To summarize, she basically took offense to the term "people who menstruate" and said that she thinks it is unsafe for society to be allowing any biological man who claims to think he is a woman into private women's areas. I do not have any issue with either of these statements, and I do not see any legitimate reason for anyone else to have issues with them either. I am sure I disagree with Rowling on many many issues, but she has a right to have her own opinion. This is just one issue where I happen to agree with her stance.

I have brought up both of these statements to basically say, neither of them has much weight for what I am discussing here. Whether you like J.K. Rowling or not, I think you can still view her accomplishments and learn from her story and struggle. Which If I am being honest is pretty remarkable. So with that stage set, let's look at her story.

One of the first things I noticed from studying the life of J.K. Rowling was that she really was incredibly gifted at taking negatives of any kind, not just failures, and turning them into something positive or product. We really see the culmination of this in her Harry Potter series.

The idea first came to her while she was on a train. It had actually been delayed and she ended up being stuck for four hours. While sitting there the ideas started coming to her. Characters and events. She would replay them over and over in her head. Not comfortable enough to ask anyone there for a pencil she kept the thoughts in her head and once she was able to she wrote them down. These initial parts she wrote would change pretty drastically, but they eventually became what many people now know and love as *The Sorcerer's Stone*. Or for all my peeps across the pond in England *The Philosopher's Stone*.

Before the book had gone anywhere Rowling's Mother passed away in 1990 due to complications with multiple sclerosis. Although this was a very tragic time, J.K. turned to her writing. Poured her emotions into that, and it shows. For anyone that is not familiar, Harry Potter's parents are killed by the evil villian of the franchise while Harry is only a baby. Even though he is only a baby, as we go through the story we can see that the hurt he feels at the initial loss and current absence of his parents is tremendous. And Rowling did a fantastic job transferring that to words on a page. Not something that is very easy to do. There were several other setbacks that happened in Rowling's life before the eventual success of the Harry Potter franchise, but let's focus on what happened right before the success. A synopsis of the first book of Harry Potter was submitted to twelve different publishing houses who all rejected it. Then it was submitted to Bloomsbury Publishing, who thought it was good enough to sign J.K. Rowling to her first contract. From there she still needed to completely finish the first book. But she would go on to become one of the highest paid authors in history.

Now one of the most interesting, and I would even say respectable, things I found out about came after her best selling series came to a close. Rowling went on to try her hand at writing other genres, and even did so under a pseudonym. Why? She wanted honest feedback and wanted her new works to be successful because they were good on their own. Not just because they had her name on the cover. And to her credit, they appear to be very good. Now obviously it is known that Robert Galbraith was actually the pen name for J.K. Rowling, but the first book released and had great success before that was common knowledge. I think this is very respectable. She easily could have monopolized on her name and intentionally chose not to. That takes a pretty upstanding moral character in my opinion.

I am cutting Rowling's story short for the sake of space in this chapter, but her story is one of persistence and perseverance. She kept going, kept pushing, kept writing. Even ended up saying later on that she partially owes her success in Harry Potter to her unsuccessful attempts at everything else. If she had done well enough in other areas it would have drawn her focus away from writing. And I for one think the world would be just a little less well off had we never heard of "the boy who lived".

Next I want to jump back into the old testament. We are focusing on persistence here in chapter 8. There are several examples of this that I could pull from the Bible, but one really came to my mind and has stuck with me while preparing and thinking about what to put in this chapter. That is the story of Moses. Moses' story is another one that most people have at least a passing familiarity with. There are two main stories that are told about Moses to children pretty frequently in churches. The first is the story of when he was a baby. The Israelites were slaves in Egypt (this was after the time of Joseph). Pharaoh commanded that all the baby boys be thrown into the Nile river. But Moses' mother hid him so that he would be spared. Moses would end up being found by Pharaoh's daughter and taken in as her son. He grew up as Egyptian royalty, then had some complications added to his story and left Egypt. While in the Desert God spoke to Moses and told him to go tell Pharaoh to let the Israelites go.

This was not going to be a popular thing for Pharaoh to hear, since the Israelite people were slave labor and the made a big impact on the Egyptian economy. God told Moses that this was not going to be easy and Pharaoh would even resist, but in the end Israel would be free. Egypt ended up getting hit with plagues. These plagues had two main purposes. The first was to show the Israelites (who had been slaves for some 400 years) that the God that their Ancestors worshiped was alive and well. The second was to show the Egyptians that their gods were nothing. Or as the Incredible Hulk might say "Puny gods". I think it is also worth noting (if you are not already aware) there was an Egyptian god for almost everything, and some of the gods were gods of multiple things.

The first plague that hit Egypt was turning the Nile river to blood. There were a couple of gods that the Egyptians associated with the Nile, and it was also believed to be the bloodstream of Osiris. The Nile turning into blood instantly caused hardship for the Egyptian economy since the fish that were in the river died and the water was unusable.

The second plague brought frogs up from the Nile. This was an attack against Heqet the frog headed goddess of birth. The ancient Egyptians believed that frogs were sacred and you were not allowed to kill them. But God sent the frogs into every part of the house for the Egyptians. Then when the frogs died their bodies were stacked into piles all across the land.

The third plague was gnats. This one was an attack against Seth (pronounced Set). Seth was the god of the desert. Pharaoh had magicians in his court that had been able to duplicate the first and second plague. But when the plague of gnats came they could not copy it, and they told Pharaoh "This is the finger of God" (Exodus 8:19)

The fourth plague was of flies. This was an attack against the Egyptian god of flies uatchit. I am gonna be real honest, your guess is as good as mine on how to pronounce that. I have heard a couple different ways. But I usually say it like you are saying the letter U then the letter H. In this plague swarms of flies went all over Egypt, except where the Israelites lived.

Here is where it starts to get serious (you know, because a river of blood isn't serious). The fifth plague was the death of livestock. This was an attack against Hathor who was the goddess of livestock. This is also the second plague where there is a distinction between Egypt and the Israelites. While the Egyptian cattle all died, the Israeli cattle were left alone. Now that we are halfway through notice that God is making a distinction. Not only does he have the power to do anything he wants but he can simultaneously give punishment to one group and prosperity to another. All while they are in the same area.

The sixth plague was boils. This one again was an attack against multiple Egyptian Gods, but among them are Sekhmet and Isis. These boils actually caused Pharaoh's Magicians to not be able to stand in front of him. So even more than an attack simply against Sekhmet and Isis, this was also a statement against those who were performing for these false gods on Pharaoh's behalf.

Before the final plagues God gave a message to Pharaoh. You can find it around Exodus 9:16, but God told Pharaoh that the final plagues would be more severe. God also told Pharaoh that he was placed in his position by God himself. This was done so that God could show his power and have his name declared through all the earth. God also warned Pharaoh and the Egyptians to take whatever cattle and crops they had remaining and shelter them before the upcoming storm. Some of the Egyptians listened to this warning, but some did not.

The seventh plague was hail. This was an attack against Nut (the sky goddess), Osiris (the crop fertility god), and Seth (the god of chaos and storms). This hail was not just normal hail. It was the worst storm that had ever hit Egypt since the land had become a nation. Like the previou plagues the hail damaged everywhere except the area of Goshen, where the Israelites lived.

The eight plague was locust. This plague was another attack against Nut, Osiris, and Seth. This was significant because the Egyptians had crops of wheat and rye that had survived the hail. These were devoured by the locusts.

The ninth plague was darkness. This was an attack against Ra who was the sun god. This was also more aggressive because Ra was symbolized by Pharaoh himself. For three whole days that land of Egypt was completely covered by darkness. No one could see anything. But once again the Israelites land was not affected.

The tenth and final plague was the death of the first born male. This was an attack against Isis, who was considered to be the protector of children. And this plague was a little different for the Israelites as well. With previous plagues Israel did not have to do anything in order to not be affected. But with this one there was an active participation required. This was also going to be a flash forward to the sacrifice required from Jesus. Each family was told to take a spotless male lamb and sacrifice it. They were to smear its blood on the top and sides of the door post. Then the lamb's meat was to be roasted and the family was to eat it that night. This is important because any family that did not do this would not be safe from the coming judgment. But any family that did this would have this plague "passover" their homes. The Israelites were saved from this, but the Egyptians were not.

This was the straw that finally broke the camel's back. Pharaoh told Moses to start gettin' while the gettin' was good. Obviously that is a bit of a paraphrase (still more accurate than the passion translation though). But Pharaoh did send the Israelites away. Now there is much more to this story and it gets even more miraculous, if that is even imaginable, but I am going to stop our recap here. For the purposes I am trying to achieve I want to focus again on persistence.

It is pretty easy to write off Moses' persistence as being simple because he had heard directly from God. But I do not think that makes it any less remarkable. Even if it were a situation where God told you specifically what was going to happen, and it started to unfold in exactly that manner, it would not be easy to continue following the instructions given when the only door through which you can go is constantly being shut in your face. Especially seeing how amazing the plagues were. The overwhelming and awesome power of the God of Israel on display for everyone to see, yet Pharaoh remained unmoved. To face that nine times, but still keep going back could not have been an easy task. And it would have taken a great amount of faith. But Moses persisted. And now we are able to read about his heroic faith and about the God that was present, even in the wilderness.

So I have a confession to make. I have never really been much of a reader. Or honestly a writer for that matter. Like I said previously, this whole book really did start as a self depreciation joke about myself. I felt like there was only one thing I could count on myself doing, and that is failing. I could definitely count on myself to do that. And it was really pertaining to everything I did or tried to do. Personally and professionally. It did not matter. I was definitely good at not being good.

One of the things I have tried my hand at with next to no success is podcasting. And that is about as narrow as I can be with it. I have tried to do a sports podcast. No bueno. A political podcast. Second-rate at best. Finally I thought I started hitting my stride during covid though. Actually started a podcast with a friend about..... Well basically just being a nerd. We talked about star wars, the walking dead, as well as plenty of other shows and things that we both really liked. And it actually wasn't doing terribly at first. But I had some issues pop up that made me have to call it quits. But I am not done with that yet. Well maybe the nerdy stuff I will keep private, but I am actually planning to launch another new podcast shortly. Called Biblically Basic, it will look at everyday topics that Christians have to face and try to examine how to handle it Biblically. Also try to focus somewhat heavily on discipleship, which is something I think is lacking in the church today. But now that the shameless self promotion is out of the way (don't judge, it's my book).

Another activity that I excelled at being terrible at (even if only in my own mind) was writing. Several different types of writing. I mentioned in the first chapter that I have written many song lyrics. I have also thrown away many song lyrics. I actually still remember lyrics I wrote to a song when I was roughly eleven or twelve years old. You see my sister and I grew up on the mean streets of a midwestern Illinois town. We were also raised on DC Talk. Then to add even more inspiration I had just been exposed to TobyMac's Momentum CD. We actually wrote a rap/ hip hop song. I think we wrote a couple but I only remember one. And I can still remember the horrifically terrible lyrics that I wrote all those years ago.

Aside from the masterfully crafted verses in my past I have also tried my hand at writing books before. I can remember some details of a couple of different books that I have attempted to write. I feel like I am really good at coming up with a general idea for a story, but just really terrible when it comes to writing. Showing detail rather than just telling what the reader sees is very difficult, especially when you are trying to do so consistently over the course of several tens of thousands of words. I do still have those ideas floating around in my head though and I may revisit them again one day, but they have also caused me a great deal of frustration.

One of the storys was going to be a sci-fi / post apocalyptic story. Honestly very Stephen King esque. The main event of the book that throws everything into motion was going to take place on an airplane. But the story started with the main character sitting in the airport waiting to board the plane. I only ended up writing a few hundred words for that story, but I can honestly say that section of writing was probably the best fiction writing I had ever done. The issue that came from that though, is that nothing after that was good enough. I would try to write and continue the story, then shortly after I would decide that what I wrote was hot garbage and delete it.

That is part of what led into this book starting. Writing out a list of all the things I have started and did not finish. All the things that I felt I had failed at. All the ways I could not measure up. Then I noticed something as I was compiling this list. I have learned a lot as a result of those failures. I am not terribly old (32 at the time of writing this chapter) but I have experienced and been through much more than a lot of people around my age. I am not implying that I was wise and sought out good opportunities to gain experience or anything like that. On the contrary. I am plainly stating that I have been incredibly stupid and made incredibly stupid decisions. But those decisions have taught me a great deal about what not to do. About how to be better. About how to fail properly. Don't just do it and move on. Look back on it and learn from it.

Through the course of writing this book I have had that same frustration pop up several times. There are parts that I have written and thought were really good. There have also been parts I have written that I thought were really bad. Sometimes I have allowed myself to try and rework a certain part. But I did not allow myself to get too hung up on one specific part. If I tried writing it out a couple of times and still could not get the words down in a way that I liked I just moved on. Allowed myself to continue on and go back to it later.

I also have others going through this with me and their feedback will be important. They may see things that I loved and they may not like it. Or things that I hated they may think sounds good. But this is going back to the first chapter, I am not doing this on my own. I have a team that is helping me and I am taking their input on everything and at the very least considering it because I know they are trying to help me in this process.

Chapter 9

What Doesn't Kill You...

This is probably going to be the least known story of any of the stories I tell in this book. But if I am being honest it is probably one of the most, if not the most, remarkable ones. I was actually not even aware of this story until I was discussing this book with a couple of guys from my Thursday night men's Bible study. Chris piped up and said "oh you have to talk about Louis Braille". Then proceeded to tell me the story. So I want to say thank you to Chris.

Louis Braille is probably the one historical figure that I have the least in total to say about. However, he is also quite possibly the one that has the most remarkable story. His early childhood is not really all that remarkable. A fairly normal childhood Louis was born in 1809. But at the age of three in 1812 Louis had an accident. While playing in his fathers workshop he got a hold of a tool called an awl. They typically are a rounded wooden handle with a shaft of sharp, pointed metal jutting out of them. Louis ended up damaging his eye with this tool.

He ended up losing his sight in that eye very quickly. There was no medical knowledge at the time that could save it. But to make matters worse, his eye would get infected and that infection spread to his other eye. By the age of five Louis Braille was completely blind.

But that did not stop him. Braille pushed through his circumstances and ended up getting a scholarship to France's Royal Institute for blind youth. Now during the time when he was attending the method for blind people to read was much different than what we have now. Nothing more than raised letters on a page. So Louis began working on something different. A way to read that was better, and much more efficient.

By the age of 15 Louis had basically completed his Braille system for reading. The first edition was published in 1829. Braille had taken a form of military code called night writing. It was a system of dots and dashes that soldiers could read safely with their fingers on the battlefield at night. This System had twelve raised dots split up into two vertical columns of six dots each. Louis simplified the system to only be six raised dots split up into two vertical columns of three dots each. This made it the perfect size for a finger tip to feel with a single touch.

Now as miraculous as this story is already there was something else that really made it stand out to me. The tool that Louis used to make these raised dots. It was an awl. Yep, he took the same thing that actually caused the condition he was suffering from and turned it around. This is truly awl inspiring (see what I did there? Sorry I had to sneak in a dad joke). But in awl seriousness (ok I am done for real now) this is absolutely amazing. Just to not only have the opportunity to turn this around, but actually have the wisdom, humility, whatever you want to call it to do so.

Braille is read from right to left and it is not its own language, more like a system of writing or code. This makes it much more easily adaptable to other languages. Because communicating words was not enough, Braille went on to make a system for math using his new method. Then, because he was a fan of music, he made a system for music using this method as well.

There is a sad part to his story however. The medical community was very slow to make any changes and Louis died at the age of 43. That was two years before the system he created was taught at the institute where he had been a student.

His system eventually spread throughout all of the French speaking world. In 1882 it had been adopted by most of Europe. And had reached the United States by 1916. The universal Braille code for English was finalized in 1932.

Even before I knew this story I would notice all the places where I see Braille lettering. Elevators, Vending machine buttons, signage at office buildings and museums. It has really always fascinated me at how many places you can find this at. And there has been part of me that has been curious to learn it as well. Maybe after learning this I will take the time to do so.

But after learning the origins of it, I am even more amazed by it. Anytime I go anywhere and see those raised bumps that signify specific letters, numbers, words, or anything else. I hope it always serves as a reminder to me, but anyone else who reads this book or knows this story. A reminder that sometimes you can take the weapons that have been used against you. Used to harm you. To take things away from you. And turn them around for good. The bible actually specifically addresses this, but it is even better. It is not just our ability to occasionally do this. I believe I have already brought up Romans 8:28 in this book, but I will do it again because it is just that good. We know that God causes EVERYTHING to work together for good. But there is a caveat at the end. You must love God, and be called according to his purpose. This doesn't mean that people who do not fit those two categories can't have negatives turn into a positive. It simply means that because I do fall into those categories, I do not have to worry about it. Times may be tough. Sucky situations may arise, but God's got it. And no matter what gets thrown at me, he can turn it around. There is a saying, that you will know if you grew up in church, but you probably won't if you did not. It sums up this idea and I will end this section with it. God is good, all the time. And all the time, God is good!

So I am going to do things a little differently in the final chapter. I want to look at my personal story and end with the Biblical. But similar to chapter 6 previously, I do not have a specific instance I want to focus on. Rather a general concept I have noticed throughout my life. There is a recurring theme that continues to pop up in my personal story. I usually do not notice it at the moment. And more often than not it is something that never even occurs to me until I am looking back on a past situation with present knowledge.

It is the promise outlined in Romans 8:28. God makes all things work together for good, for those who love him and are called according to his purpose. There are things that happen to us that are not directly caused by God. Free will and having the opportunity to choose whether or not to follow God is an amazing gift, but it also opens the door for a lot of very bad things. God never promises that we will not have bad things happen to us. He never promises that we will not have trouble in this life either. He actually says the exact opposite. Jesus said people would hate us for our faith in him because they hated him first. But God does promise that he can bring good out of every situation.

I know by even bringing up this topic I am infuriating some people and quite possibly opening a giant can of worms. And not normal worms. I am talking like Graboids from Tremors. Just the nature of talking about bad things happening to people can be difficult and bring out a lot of emotion. But I can stand firm on the fact that I know this is a principle completely backed by the Bible. And I would ask that if you have made it this far, let me talk through this before you write me off.

I am not saying that everything that happens to a christian is good. Far from it. Jesus actually promises us that we will have troubles in this world. And specifically that people would hate us because they hated him first. I am saying God can turn anything around and use it for good. Yes, anything. Now to illustrate this point I am going to incorporate a little bit of apologetics here. There are things that happen on this earth that do not seem to have any positive outcome. Or no way that anyone, even God could turn it around to be beneficial. But if we are agreeing to the fact that God exists, even if only for this argument, we must also agree that he is infinitely more knowledgeable than we are or could ever hope to be.

I know people who are against this instantly jump to the worst possible situation, so I will jump to one of them myself. Pediatric Cancer. If God really existed he would not allow that, right? Or if He does allow it, he just is not all good like we claim. I would like to draw a comparison to another situation. But before I do please understand that I am not equating this situation to having cancer or any other horrible situation someone may find themselves in. I am simply telling an anecdotal story to illustrate a point.

I have an eight month old daughter, she has had to get shots recently. Now for her, this is the worst thing she has ever experienced. Not only is it the worst pain she has felt in her entire life, but her dad is actually holding her down and allowing it to happen. This situation is very real and breaks my heart every time it has happened. But it is necessary. No matter how I may try to explain it, my daughter will never understand. This pain may be horrible right now, but there is a benefit to it. One day she will not even remember the pain she went through, but she will know that she never had Polio. Never even had to worry about Polio. I can try as much as I want to explain that to her, but she will never understand me. But her level of understanding is so far below anything that would be able to understand that concept. This situation is similar to ours. The biggest difference I would say though is that my eight month old is far closer to my level of knowledge than anyone is to God's

I have experienced this in my own life as well. I talked in a previous chapter about my struggles with porn. That was not something I chose for myself. I did not go searching for it. But it found me. Was thrown on me and I never stood a chance. I battled that for over a decade. Finally got free. And now, I have seen my story be a beacon of hope for others. And more than that, I have used what I went through to help others find success in breaking free from this as well. This is a situation that I have actually been able to understand and see the positive outcome from in this life. But that is not always the case.

I experienced death for the first time at a fairly young age and it was pretty personal. I am not going to go into a lot of detail out of respect for the family, but I will share what I feel I can. I was twelve years old, and I had a very close friend. We played sports together all throughout the school year. It took me a long time to cope with the death of my friend. Especially knowing how it happened and being able to see it play over and over again in my mind. It was a very gruesome situation. For years I struggled with this. And I hated myself for several things surrounding this situation. But the one I struggled with the most was I never once talked to him about Jesus. Now I know his family was religious. They went to church regularly and he would have known probably just as much as I did. But I had a serious complex about this for a long time and it messed me up for a very long time. I have not yet in this life seen a positive come out of this situation. And if I am being honest, I do not know that I ever will. But I look forward to hopefully seeing my friend again one day, and being able to eventually see what God did through this.

The next Bible figure I would like to look at someone we have already examined a little bit. We've discussed Jacob in two separate chapters, so I do not see an issue doing that again with King David. Actually this is prior to his kingship. But after he had been anointed by Samuel. We have seen David as a Shepherd boy, and we saw David as King. This story takes place in between. And if you ever attended church as a child you have probably heard this story. Although I am a little lost as to why it is told to children. I could say the same about Noah and the ark... but I am actually planning to talk about that in a later chapter.

The armies of Israel and the armies of the Philistines are gathered to battle. David had three older brothers who were there to fight. Jesse, David's father, told David to take some food to his brothers on the battlefield. When he did he walked into quite a surprise. Prior to David arriving there was this one particular Philistine named Goliath that was causing quite a problem for Israel. Goliath is described as having a height of six cubits and a span. This is roughly nine foot and nine inches tall.

Alright, that is a little crazy. I mean I am six foot tall (as long as I remember to stand up straight and have good posture). I have a friend who plays basketball professionally in Canada. He is 6ft 9in tall. And he is considerably taller than I am. Like very very noticeable. I cannot even imagine seeing someone almost ten feet tall.

Back to Goliath though. For 40 days he would come out in front of the army of Israel and the following would happen. Check out 1 Samuel 17: 8-11.

[8]Goliath stood and shouted to the ranks of Israel, "why do you come out and line up for battle? Am I not a Philistine, and are you not the servants of Saul? Choose a man and have him come down to me. [9]If he is able to fight and kill me, we will become your subjects; but if I overcome him and kill him, you will become our subjects and serve us." [10]Then the Philistine said, "This day I defy the armies of Israel! Give me a man and let us fight each other."

[11]On hearing the Philistine's words, Saul and all the Israelites were dismayed and terrified.

So for 40 days he taunted and for 40 days no one so much as said a word to him. That is until David showed up. Everyone was afraid except for David. David asks what will be done for the man who kills Goliath, then starts asking "Who is this uncircumcised Philistine that he should defy the armies of the living God?" That may sound a little strange. But back in the day, this was David hurling insults.

Word ends up getting back to Saul about what David was saying and Saul calls for David. They have a little bit of a back and forth about the matter. Saul first tells David he could never fight Goliath. But David disputes him and Saul very quickly changes his mind. I personally think this was more an effort on Sauls part to see how serious David was, rather than trying to dissuade him from attempting to fight.

Saul initially dresses David up in his armor and gear for war, but they were not working for David because he was not used to them. I imagine that while in a life or death situation you will probably want to be familiar with the tools you are using, both for offense and defense. I mean, I have never personally done it, but I feel that I can make an educated guess on the matter.

It is also important to know that this would not be David's first time fighting for his life. He actually brings this up to Saul as well, but as a Shepherd he had to fight off Lions and Bears(No Tigers, OH MY!). When they would come get a sheep, he would chase it down get the sheep back, and kill the wild animal. He said this "Uncircumcised Philistine" is going to be no different. So David leaves, and goes to get five smooth stones for his sling.

Goliath sees David and starts mocking him. Not only does he not have armor but he doesn't have a sword either. I have read and listened to some commentary on this chapter. Many scholars seem to think that Goliath actually must have had a helmet on. Then in this moment when he starts laughing at David, his helmet falls off. Goliath is yelling some insults at David and David yells back. But David is not coming against Goliath in his own strength. David knows where the strength is coming from and it makes it known to Goliath and everyone else there that day. He says clearly that God will deliver Goliath into his hands.

I can think of a situation that would be somewhat similar. I love basketball. One of my favorite sports to watch and I enjoy playing it quite a bit. Now, I am a pretty humble guy, but I need to be honest about this. I have completely dominated basically every game I have played for the last couple of years. Pay no attention to the fact that those games have been against my now 11 year old son.

Anyways, this Goliath situation would be like if I was going to play 3 on 3 with some local kids, but I had MJ and Shaq both in the prime of their career as the other two on my team. It really does not matter how good, or bad I may be. My teammates are really really good. So you best believe I am gonna be talking some trash. Like A LOT of trash talk. I am a competitive person, and I like to talk trash (My wife hates it). And any athlete worth their salt knows it is much easier to talk trash when you know you, or in this situation your team, can back it up. But it is not at all because I think my efforts are going to lead to the win, I do however know the team that I have backing up what I am saying. And I know with prime MJ and Shaq on my team, playing against local kids, they can back up whatever trash I wanna talk. But in David's case, it is an even better backup than what I would have.

So Goliath starts charging at David, and David does the same. David pulls one of the stones out and with his sling he lobs it at Goliath. The stone sinks into Goliath's forehead and stops him right in his tracks. Now we are getting to the point I really want to focus on for this story. As Goliath lay there on the ground David finishes the job. He walks up and cuts off the head of Goliath. With Goliath's own sword. So the weapon that Goliath was planning on using to kill David, ends up getting turned around to secure victory for David.

This is actually a fairly common theme throughout the Bible. Joseph directly acknowledges this with his brothers when addressing them. He says "what you intended for harm, God used for good". But Joseph could have said this in several circumstances throughout his life. How about Potiphar's wife? I would say it is pretty clear she had some nefarious intentions to say the least.

One I have not discussed yet, but we will in a later chapter is Moses. While Israel was held captive as slaves in Egypt Pharoh ordered that all the first born males be killed. So Moses' mother tried hiding him, when she no longer could, she put him in a basket and set him in the Nile river in a spot where she knew Pharaoh's daughter went in hopes that she would take him in. That is exactly what happens and that sets the path for Moses to…… I better stop, because I will go into more detail with this later. But the point is, what was intended for evil, God used for good.

Then we have Paul, whom we already discussed. He definitely had some negative intentions for the early church. However, God had other plans. He had the first Damascus road experience and ended up writing a majority of the New Testament that we have today. And honestly reshaping the world forever.

And finally we have the most obvious and most important example. Jesus. I am not going to go super deep on theology, but I do feel it is important to provide a proper understanding of the christian faith here for a couple reasons.

The first is, I believe it to be Truth. Not just a truth, but THE ABSOLUTE TRUTH. So much so that, to quote NF again, "If God ain't real, real isn't" While writing this book I am hoping that it does reach people that have never stepped foot inside of a church building, or that have been hurt by church people, or that for whatever reason have rejected Christianity and the Christian God. And I hope that maybe my experiences or something I wrote will at the very least make you want to give it another chance. I will be the first to admit that there are many times that people suck. But God is always good, even if we do not see it in the moment, or in this lifetime.

Secondly is to help you understand the situation that is going on when I mention Jesus. I believe in the Trinity. That is 1 God, that is made up of 3 distinct persons. For times sake I am going to not go any further into that, but just grant me this premise for the purpose of what I am going to say. Jesus was God. Not a hippie. Not just some prophet. Not even just a nice guy. He was God. And still is for that matter. But when he came to earth and was born of a virgin he became a man. Took on human flesh, but retained his Godliness too. Fully God, fully man. The Jewish leaders of the day hated Jesus because he turned everything they had spent their lives studying, teaching, and proclaiming on its head. And on top of that, he called them out on several occasions. In front of people too. One instance called them "white washed tombs", they look good on the outside, but they are full of dead men's bones. Jesus made a lot of people mad when he came the first time. So much so that a conspiracy was hatched to get him executed. And it worked.

I imagine on that day, Lucifer and his demons were pretty excited. They knew who Jesus was. I believe they had a hand in getting the crowds riled up enough to chant for his crucifixion, when he had done nothing wrong. Then as he hung on the cross between two thieves He cried out "Father, into your hands I commit my spirit" and He died. The rejoicing that must have come forth from all of Satan's followers must have been overwhelming. Then three days later, something unexpected happened. Jesus was resurrected. This is attested to by some 500 eyewitnesses. Most atheist New Testament scholars do not even dispute that these people believe they actually saw Jesus. The best explanation they can give for this is mass hallucination.

But why is this so important? Because this death was supposed to be final. And it was actually supposed to be ours. Death and eternity in hell is the punishment for sin. All sin. There are no different levels. But Jesus became a man, with the sole purpose of being crucified, going to hell, defeating death, and coming back so that we could spend eternity with him. The requirements to receive this gift are pretty simple too, they are clearly outlined in Romans 10. You must confess with your mouth that Jesus is Lord, and believe in your heart that God raised him from the dead. That is all it takes. Now there will be changes in your life, those are a result of the change in your heart. But for actual salvation, what I have listed is all that is needed. Seems too good to be true, but there is actually quite a bit of evidence suggesting that the Bible is in fact true.

If the Bible is true, that means Jesus is God, and gets back to the previous point I made.

Conclusion

If you are reading this then that means you made it to the end. Congratulations! You do not win anything though. But in all seriousness I did want to say thank you. I appreciate the time that was spent reading this book. And I do honestly hope that it was as fun, entertaining, fulfilling for you to read as it was for me to write.

I believe the concept that I have been trying to detail in this book is one that everyone can learn from and learn to use. I listed many different individuals in this book that managed to push through failure to find success. That comes in many different ways, and probably will not look the same at every stage of your life. I do believe though that there is one thing you can do in order to set your life up for this. And it may be cliche, but I am going to say it anyway because it is true. Placing God at the front and center of your life is the best step you can make.

I am not suggesting that doing this will instantly make everything sunshine and rainbows. On the contrary, I think you are even more likely to go through struggles in this world as a result of making this decision. Jesus even reassures us of this saying the world will hate us because they hated him first. And yes I believe things in this world to have a purpose and do matter. But the real success, the success that actually matters, is going to be eternal. The ultimate way for you to know you made it is to hear the words "well done my good and faithful servant". One day we will all either hear that or be told to depart.

I earnestly hope that when that day comes I will see you there. And then you can tell me personally how I could have made this book better. If you have enjoyed this book feel free to look up some of my other projects. I will have a list in the back of this book that should help point you in the right direction. God Bless!

Don't miss out!

Visit the website below and you can sign up to receive emails whenever Jesse Lucas publishes a new book. There's no charge and no obligation.

https://books2read.com/r/B-A-GNKX-TJLQC

BOOKS2READ

Connecting independent readers to independent writers.

Printed in the USA
CPSIA information can be obtained
at www.ICGtesting.com
JSHW010036090224
56972JS00012B/146